FAT QUARTER

QUICK MAKES

25 projects to make from short lengths of fabric

Juliet Bawden & Amanda Russell

First published 2017 by
Guild of Master Craftsman Publications Ltd
Castle Place, 166 High Street, Lewes,
East Sussex, BN7 1XU

Publisher Jonathan Bailey
Production Manager Jim Bulley
Senior Project Editor Sara Harper
Editor Cath Senker
Managing Art Editor Gilda Pacitti
Art Editor Luana Gobbo
Photographer Rowland Roques-O'Neil
Step photography Studio of R&B Designs
Picture credit Cover illustrations: Shutterstock/Ohn Mar

Colour origination by GMC Reprographics
Printed and bound in Turkey

A note on measurements

The imperial measurements in these projects are
converted from metric. While every attempt has been
made to ensure that they are as accurate as possible,
some rounding up or down has been inevitable. For
this reason, it is always best to stick to one system
or the other throughout a project: do not mix metric
and imperial units.

CONTENTS

INTRODUCTION

Both of us have always enjoyed sewing, and from an early age we were making clothes for dolls and teddies. We soon progressed to household items and gifts for family and friends, and from there to making our own clothes for everyday and special occasions. If, like us, you are addicted to creating, then you are bound to have a stash of fabric in glorious patterns and colours just waiting to be used. There are always remnants left over from projects, as well as those must-have, impulse-buy fat quarters of fabrics you spot when you're out and about. In this book we've designed 25 fabulous projects that will help you transform these oddments into stylish and individual items in a flash. And nowadays with the emphasis on looking after the environment, it's also immensely rewarding to feel that you're helping to make the most of resources while creating something lovely from leftover bits and pieces.

Projects are organized under the following themes: fashion & accessories, baby & child, out & about, workroom and presents. They range from a cute baby's dress to practical but pretty storage solutions such as a tent tidy, with lots of other useful and decorative items in between. Each project can either be made from fat quarters, or from remnants pieced together. A fat quarter is simply half a yard of fabric cut in half again vertically, and in this book it refers to an 18 x 22in (46 x 56cm) maximum piece of fabric. Sizes do vary, depending upon the width from which the fabric is cut, so bear this in mind when working out your fabric requirements.

This book is aimed at those with some basic sewing skills, and as a source of inspiration for those with more sewing experience. A sewing machine is useful but you can also make most of the projects by hand if you don't have one. All of the projects are very quick and easy, with simple instructions and step-by-step images to help you achieve great results. We hope you have as much fun making them as we did.

Juliet and Amanda

THE BASICS

MATERIALS AND EQUIPMENT

We like to keep things simple, so our list of essential tools mostly consists of items you will already have. For a few projects you will need additional equipment, such as D handles for the knitting bag.

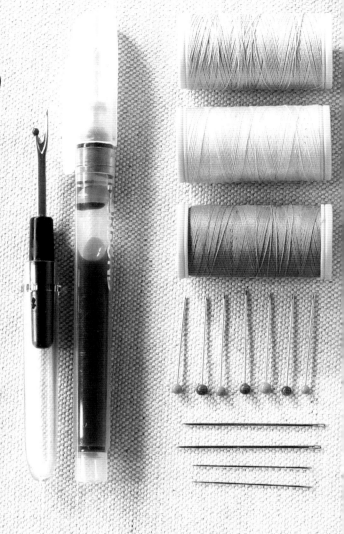

SCISSORS Sharp scissors are a must: a large pair of dress-making scissors for cutting fabric and a smaller pair for detailed tasks such as cutting threads. Keep a different pair for cutting paper, which blunts scissors. Label your scissors so you know which is which!

SEAM RIPPER This handy tool is essential for quick and easy unpicking if you need to correct mistakes in your sewing.

PINS Glass-headed pins are the most suitable to use. With their bold colours, they are visible, easy to pick up, a good length and will pierce fabric readily.

NEEDLES Make sure you have a selection of small and large needles needles, as well as thicker embroidery needles, for hand sewing.

SEWING MACHINE You will need a sewing machine that does straight stitching and zigzag for the projects, though you can make everything by hand if you don't have one. Store your sewing machine in its case and to keep it performing well, have it serviced regularly. Sharp needles are a must, so keep a stash, and when you start a project replace the existing needle with one the correct width for the fabric you are using. Always test out your machine stitch size and tension on a scrap of the fabric you are working with before starting on your project and adjust if necessary.

TAPE MEASURE AND RULER Nothing beats a dress-making tape measure with both metric and imperial measurements. A ruler is useful for smaller jobs.

PENS, PENCILS AND TRACING PAPER A water-erasable marker pen is essential for marking fabric. It is really simple to use and you can remove the marks later with a burst of steam while ironing. Have pens, pencils and tracing paper or baking parchment ready for drawing paper patterns.

IRON AND IRONING BOARD Buy the best steam iron you can afford. It makes all the difference to the finish of a project to iron as you go along, ironing after each step you have completed. Your ironing board should be firm and stable with a clean, well padded cover.

SAFETY PINS Use safety pins for threading elastic and ribbon through casings.

FABRICS You can often buy ends of rolls and remnants of designer fabrics for a fraction of their original price. The projects in this book have been made up in cotton fabric but most fabrics are suitable to use. Mix and match oddments to make up different lengths if you don't have enough of one particular fabric. Make sure you always prewash fabric to avoid problems with shrinking later.

INTERFACING If the fabric for a project needs to be thicker and more substantial, for a simple solution iron fusible interfacing or fleece to the reverse side.

THREAD Cotton thread is strong and firm, and comes in a rainbow of colours. A neutral colour is useful and can be used for different projects. It's also wise to have a range of sewing machine bobbins loaded with different-coloured threads, ready for your projects.

GENERAL HABERDASHERY Lift your project out of the ordinary by choosing the details carefully. Start looking in unusual places for essentials: often stationery and homeware stores will have good additions to your stash. You can also adapt other materials to find the look you desire. For example, coloured elastic might be difficult to find but bright hair elastics can be cut and used instead. You will also need buttons, foam ties, bias binding, press studs, wadding and toy stuffing to finish the projects.

TECHNIQUES

Life's too short for complicated techniques, which is why all the projects in this book use simple ones. Most stitching in the projects is done on a sewing machine using straight or zigzag stitch, but you could also sew them by hand if you don't have a sewing machine. You will need to hand sew openings used for turning work.

STRAIGHT STITCH

The most basic of machine stitches, use straight stitch to join two pieces of fabric together and for top stitching and attaching binding.

ZIGZAG STITCH

This machine stitch is used for neatening raw edges to reduce fraying and for decorative effects such as appliqué (see the Appliqué Patch project, page 32). Adjust the stitch width for a narrower or wider zigzag and the stitch length to determine how close together the stitches will be.

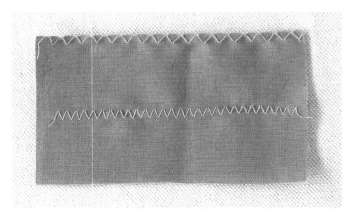

RUNNING STITCH

This is the most basic hand stitch of all. Bring the needle out to the right side of the work. Then push the needle in and out of the fabric. Aim to make each stitch and each gap between stitches the same length.

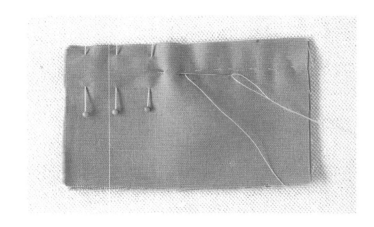

TACKING

Tacking (or basting) is a large running stitch that is used to hold two pieces of fabric in place temporarily when pins would get in the way. It can also be used for gathering. The stitches and gaps should be about ⅜in (1cm) long.

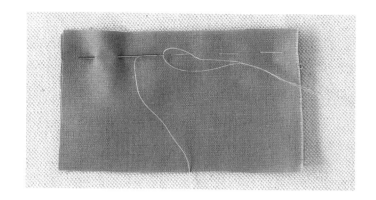

SLIP STITCH

This hand stitch can be used to join two folded edges together. It is also used to stitch hems, attach bias binding and close up gaps. When joining two folded edges, bring the needle out through one edge, then make a small stitch into the fold on the opposite edge. Pull the thread through, then make another small stitch into the fold on the opposite edge. Continue in this way, stitching into each edge in turn and pulling the thread to draw the two folds together.

CUTTING INTO A CURVE

To form a smooth line on the right side of the work, when you have a curve, it helps to cut into it. It will also allow you to press the seam flat if you need to. After stitching the seam, trim to about ¼in (6mm) and snip little V-shaped notches into the seam allowance up to the seam.

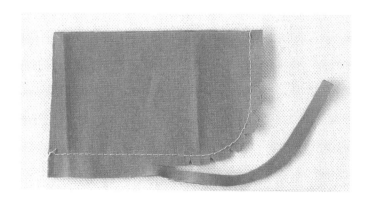

CLIPPING A CORNER

This helps to reduce bulk and keep the corners square when turning the project right sides out. When you have finished sewing the seam, snip off the corner diagonally, keeping as close to the stitches as you can.

BIAS BINDING

Binding gives a neat finish and can be less bulky than a hem. This is used for the Pillowcase Dress project on page 42 and the Bunting on page 64.

1 Open out one of the folded edges of the bias binding and place it along the edge of the fabric, with right sides together and raw edges matching. Pin in place and machine stitch together. Trim the seam and cut into the curve (see page 15).

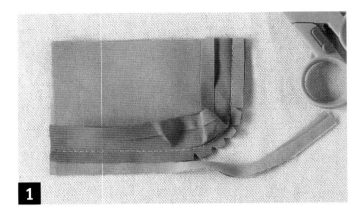

2 Fold the binding over the fabric edge to the wrong side, and line up the folded edge of the binding tape with the line of stitching. Pin in place. Using slip stitch (see page 15), stitch the folded edge of the binding to the fabric.

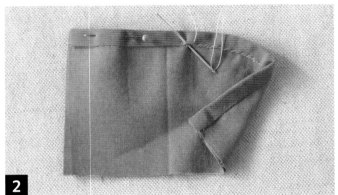

ELASTIC BUTTONHOLE

It's easy to sew a loop of elastic into a seam and it makes a great alternative to a buttonhole. This is used for the Travel Sewing Kit on page 68 and for the Pencil Case on page 98.

1 Cut the elastic to length. It will need to fit snugly around the button when fastened. Bring the two cut ends together to make a loop. With the loop facing inwards, pin the cut ends in position on the right side of the fabric.

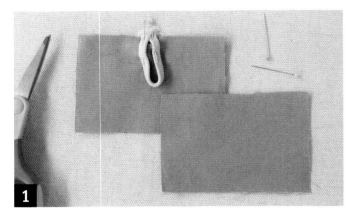

2 With right sides together, pin another piece of fabric the same size on top and sew the two pieces of fabric together to secure the buttonhole elastic. Fold the fabric right sides out and press along the seam. Avoid pressing the elastic, or it could melt.

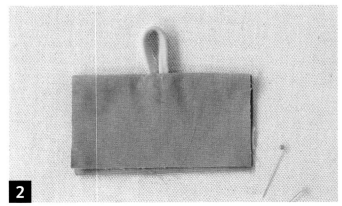

HANGING LOOP

This is a strong loop that works well for projects such as the Tent Tidy on page 60.

1 With right sides out, fold the strip of loop fabric in half lengthways. Press the fold to crease. Open out the fabric and fold in the outside edges to meet on the crease. Press this fold to crease.

2 Fold the strip in half again so all the raw edges are hidden. Pin and machine sew along the turned edge to close.

3 Fold the strip in half to form a loop. With the loop facing inwards, position it in between the two main pieces of fabric (right sides together). Pin and stitch together.

4 Turn right sides out.

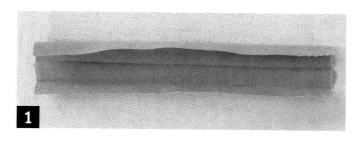

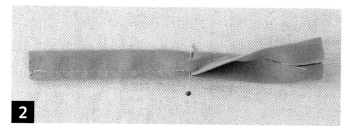

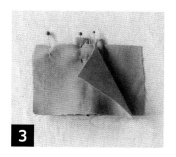
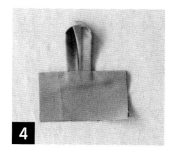

TOP STITCHING

Top stitching gives a decorative finish and holds layers neatly in place. This is used for several projects, such as the Festival Flag on page 72.

1 With wrong side facing, press the seam to one side.

2 Fold right sides out and press to crease along the seam line.

3 Machine stitch along the edge close to the fold, sewing as straight and evenly as possible.

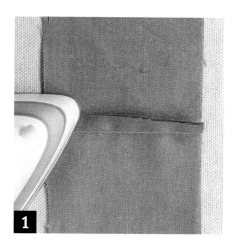

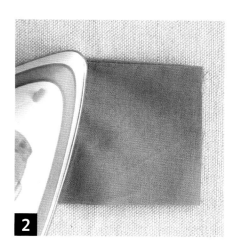

FASHION & ACCESSORIES

MOBILE PHONE COVER

It's so much nicer to make your own phone cover than to buy one. This project has a tab and carabiner so you can attach your phone to a bag, or if you have a dedicated phone pocket, you could make it without them. Use a stiff fabric for extra protection.

You will need
1 fat quarter of main fabric
1 fat quarter of lining fabric
3in (7.5cm) length of 1in (2.5cm)-wide elastic
Tracing paper or baking parchment
Pencil and ruler or tape measure
Scissors
Pins
Dress-making scissors
Sewing machine
Thread to match fabric
Sewing needle
Tape measure or ruler
Carabiner
Iron and ironing board

NOTE: You can make the whole project from one fat quarter of fabric if you use the same material for the lining.

1 Measure your mobile phone and add ¼in (6mm) to each measurement, plus ⅜in (1cm) seam allowance all the way round. Draw the measurements onto tracing paper or baking parchment and cut out to make a paper pattern.

2 Fold the fabrics in half. Pin the pattern onto the main and lining fabrics and cut out two from each fabric.

3 Make the tab by folding the elastic in half so it measures 1½ x 1in (4 x 2.5cm) and pin to hold it together.

4 With right sides facing, pin the front to the back of the main fabric, with the loop sandwiched in the side seam, facing inwards, approximately 2in (5cm) from the top. Machine sew round three sides using straight stitch (see page 14) and leave the top open. Trim the seams and clip the corners (see page 15).

5 Turn the right way and press the cover flat, but do not press the elastic, or it could melt.

6 With right sides facing, pin the front to the back of the lining. Machine sew round three sides and leave the top open. Trim the seams and clip the corners. Turn the right way out through the opening and press flat.

7 With wrong sides together, place the lining case into the main fabric (outer) case. Turn the top edge under by ⅜in (1cm) on both the inner and outer case. Pin and then machine sew through both the main fabric and lining opening.

8 Press flat, taking care not to iron the elastic. Attach the carabiner to the loop.

Tip

To make this into a phone case to carry round the neck, add loops to both sides of the case and thread a cord or ribbon through them.

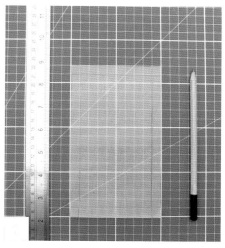

2

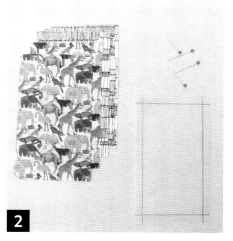

3

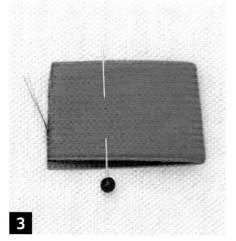

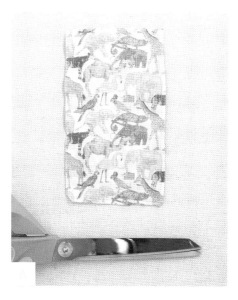

5

6

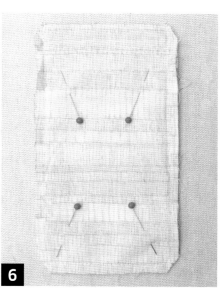

7

8

JEWELLERY ROLL

A jewellery roll really comes into its own when you are away from home, and it's great having somewhere safe to keep all your pieces together in one place. This roll has two pockets for larger items such as bracelets and necklaces, and a ring holder.

You will need
1 fat quarter of main fabric
1 fat quarter of lining fabric
6¾ x 10in (17 x 25cm) of fusible wadding
Tape measure or ruler
Iron and ironing board
Dress-making scissors
Pins
Sewing machine
Thread to match fabric
Sewing needle
Small amount of toy stuffing or wadding
Press stud

Tip
If you have more rings than other jewellery, you could make a second ring holder.

1 Cut out one 6¾ x 10in (17 x 25cm) rectangle from the main fabric and the lining fabric. Cut two 4 x 3in (10 x 7.5cm) pocket pieces and one 5½ x 2in (14 x 5cm) ring-holder piece from the main fabric.

2 Make both pockets by turning one long edge under and under again by ¼in (6mm). Press and then machine sew with a straight stitch (see page 14). Turn under the other three sides by ¼in (6mm) and press flat. Pin onto the lining fabric piece and machine sew close to the edge, leaving the opening towards the middle on the left-hand pocket and towards the outer side on the right-hand pocket.

3 Iron the fusible wadding onto the wrong side of the inner fabric, where you have just sewn the pockets.

4 Make the ring holder. With right sides facing, fold the fabric in half lengthways and machine sew with a straight stitch down one long and one short side close to the edge, leaving one side open for turning.

5 Turn right side out and fill with toy stuffing to make a long, thin sausage. Use a pair of scissors to help you do this.

6 Pin the short, unsewn edge of the ring holder to the side between the pockets. Using a needle and thread, sew one part of the press stud on the lining fabric and the other on the end of the ring holder so they can attach easily.

7 Make a tie to wrap the roll. Cut a piece of lining fabric 11 x 1¼in (28 x 3cm), fold the piece in half lengthways and press flat. Open up, fold the edges into the centre and one of the short ends in by ⅜in (1cm). Fold the piece back in half so all raw edges are hidden. Machine sew with a straight stitch close to the edge.

8 With right sides facing, pin the main (outer) fabric to the lining fabric. Make sure to sandwich the end of the ring holder in the centre of one of the long sides and pin in place. Sandwich one end of the tying tape in the centre of one of the short sides and pin in place. Make sure the tape is facing inwards. Sew around three and a quarter sides, leaving a gap of 2¼in (6cm) for turning through on the other short side. Trim the seams and clip the corners (see page 15).

9 Pull the jewellery roll right side out. Fold in the edges of the opening, press flat and slip stitch (see page 15) the opening closed with a needle and thread.

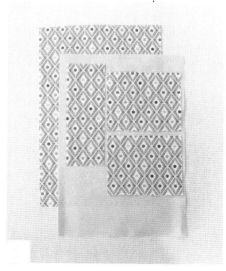

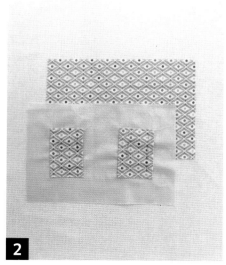

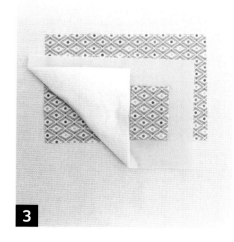

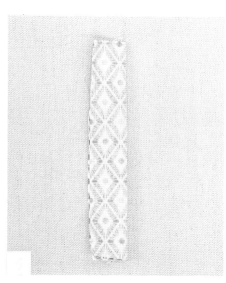

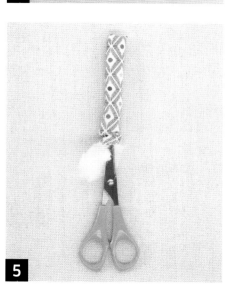

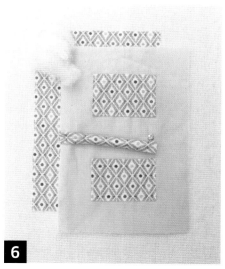

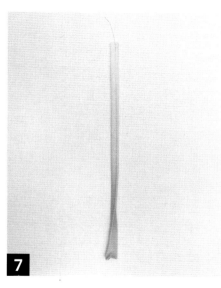

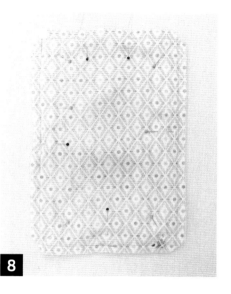

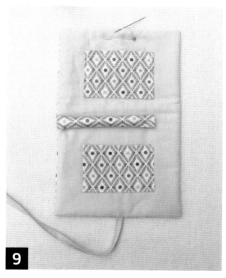

OWL BROOCH

Delve into your stash for the very smallest fabric scraps and pieces of felt to make this adorable little owl brooch. For those who prefer felines, simply adjust the facial features and create a cute cat instead: you could use black embroidery thread to make whiskers.

Find the templates on page 128

You will need
5 x 5in (12.5 x 12.5cm) of fabric
Felt scraps in white and yellow (or similar colours)
2 beads for eyes
Tracing paper or baking parchment (optional)
Pencil (optional)
Scissors
Dress-making scissors
Water-erasable pen
Tape measure or ruler
Pins
Sewing machine
Thread to match fabric
Sewing needle
Small amount of wadding
Iron and ironing board
Fabric or PVA glue
Safety pin

NOTE: This project is perfect for using up small pieces of fabric.

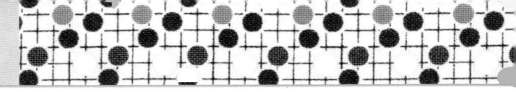

1 Photocopy or trace over the templates on page 128 and cut them out with paper-cutting scissors to make patterns. Fold the main piece of fabric in half and cut out two head shapes. Cut out two eyes in white felt and a beak in yellow.

2 Use a water-erasable pen to mark the position of the eyes and beak on the owl face.

3 Pin the head shapes right sides together. Machine sew around the edge with a ¼in (6mm) seam allowance. Sew very slowly and turn the corners with the machine needle in the down position to pivot. Leave an opening of ¾in (2cm) in the seam so that you can turn your work. Trim off the points of the ears.

4 Turn the owl head right sides out through the opening. Use the point of a pair of scissors to push out the seams and a pin to ease out the corners so that you keep the shape.

5 Take small, pea-sized pieces of wadding to stuff the head shape, pushing it into the corners with scissors or a pin.

6 Hand sew the opening closed with a needle and thread, using slip stitch (see page 15). Glue on the felt details with fabric or PVA glue. Once the glue has dried, sew on the bead eyes.

7 With a needle and thread, hand sew the back of the safety pin onto the back of the brooch. To cover the back of the safety pin, cut a piece of fabric the length of the back of the safety pin. Turn in the rough edges and press to crease. Hand sew the piece of fabric over the back of the safety pin to the back of the brooch.

Tip

Most hand stitches are worked from left to right. You may need to work in the other direction if you are left-handed.

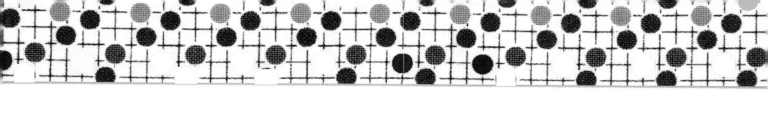

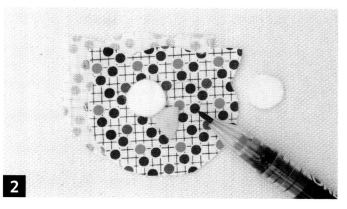

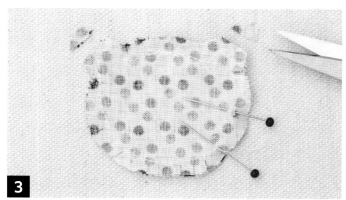

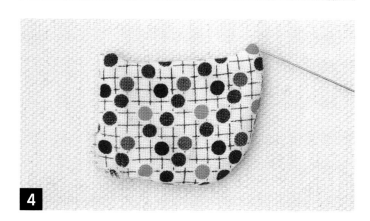

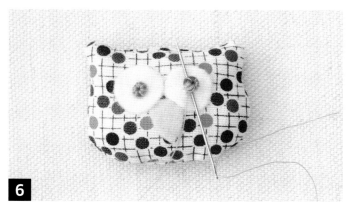

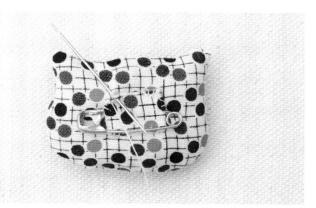

APPLIQUÉ PATCH

Patches are a brilliant way to disguise a hole in a garment, or even to turn into badges. To create a letter to embellish your patch, choose a font you like on your computer, enlarge the letter and print it. Cut it out with paper scissors to use as a template.

Find the template on page 129

You will need
1 fat quarter of main fabric for the patch
6¼ x 4¼in (16 x 11cm) of fusible wadding
4 x 2¾in (10 x 7cm) of contrast fabric for the appliqué letter
4 x 2¾in (10 x 7cm) of fusible webbing
Tracing paper or baking parchment (optional)
Pencil (optional)
Scissors
Pins
Dress-making scissors
Sewing machine
Thread to match fabric
Sewing needle
Iron and ironing board
Tape measure or ruler

NOTE: One fat quarter will make two patches.

1 Photocopy or trace over the template on page 129. Cut it out with paper-cutting scissors to make a pattern. Fold the main fabric in half, pin on the pattern and cut it out so you have two oval shapes.

2 Pin the pattern onto the fusible wadding, cut it out and press it onto the reverse of one of the pieces of fabric to make the back.

3 Iron the fusible webbing onto the back of the contrast fabric. Cut out the letter and turn it over. Draw around the reversed side onto the back of the paper side of the fusible webbing. Cut out the letter.

4 Peel off the paper backing. Press the letter onto the front piece of the patch and then machine sew round it using a zigzag stitch (see page 14).

5 With right sides together, pin the two ovals together. Machine sew around all the edges using straight stitch (see page 14) and a ³⁄₈in (1cm) seam allowance throughout. Leave an opening of 1³⁄₄in (4cm) for turning. Trim the seams then clip around the edge (see page 15).

6 Pull the patch through the opening so it is right sides out. Slip stitch the opening closed with a needle and thread (see page 15).

7 Press the patch. Sew a line of top stitching (see page 17) close to the edge to neaten.

Tip

Set your sewing machine's stitch length to 1.5, width to 3.5 and practise this stitch on scraps of fabric before you sew the letter onto the patch.

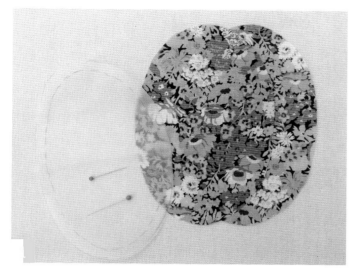

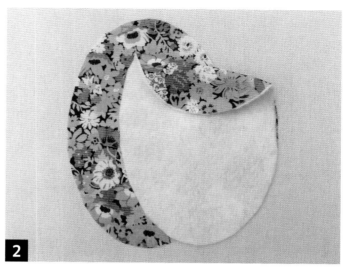

2

4

5

6

7

BABY
& CHILD

PARTY BIB

For a special meal, you want your baby to look good but he or she will still need a bib to keep clothes clean! Because the hook-and-loop fastening is on both the front and back, this bib is reversible so you can make it in fabrics to match different outfits.

Find the template on page 129

You will need
1 fat quarter of main fabric
1 fat quarter of contrast fabric
Tape measure or ruler
2in (5cm) piece of hook-and-loop fastening
60in (152cm) length of bias binding
Tracing paper or baking parchment
Pencil
Scissors
Pins
Dress-making scissors
Sewing machine
Thread to match fabric
Sewing needle
Iron and ironing board

NOTE: You can make the bib from one fat quarter of fabric if you use the same material for the whole project.

1 Photocopy the template on page 129 and trace over it onto tracing paper or baking parchment. Cut out with paper-cutting scissors to make a pattern. Place one fabric on top of the other, pin the pattern on top and then cut out the bib shape.

2 With right sides facing outwards, pin the front onto the back of the bib. Using a ⅜in (1cm) seam allowance, machine sew the front to the back using a straight stitch (see page 14). Trim round the edge of the bib so the stitching is only ¼in (6mm) from the edge.

3 Open up the bias strip and fold in the end in by ⅜in (1cm). With right sides outwards, pin one edge all the way round the edge of the bib and then machine sew together. Trim the bias strip to overlap at the join. See also Bias Binding technique, page 16.

4 Clip carefully around the curves, right up to the stitching (see page 15). The tighter the curve, the closer together the cuts need to be.

5 Fold the bias strip over the raw edges and pin and tack (see page 15) into place. Remove the pins and then machine sew with a straight stitch close to the edge. Remove the tacking.

6 Machine sew one side of the hook-and-loop fastening to the right side of the bib as indicated on the pattern. Sew the other piece to the other side. Repeat on the inside of the bib to make the bib reversible. Press to finish.

Tip

It is sometimes easier to tack, rather than pin, bias binding in place before sewing it with the machine.

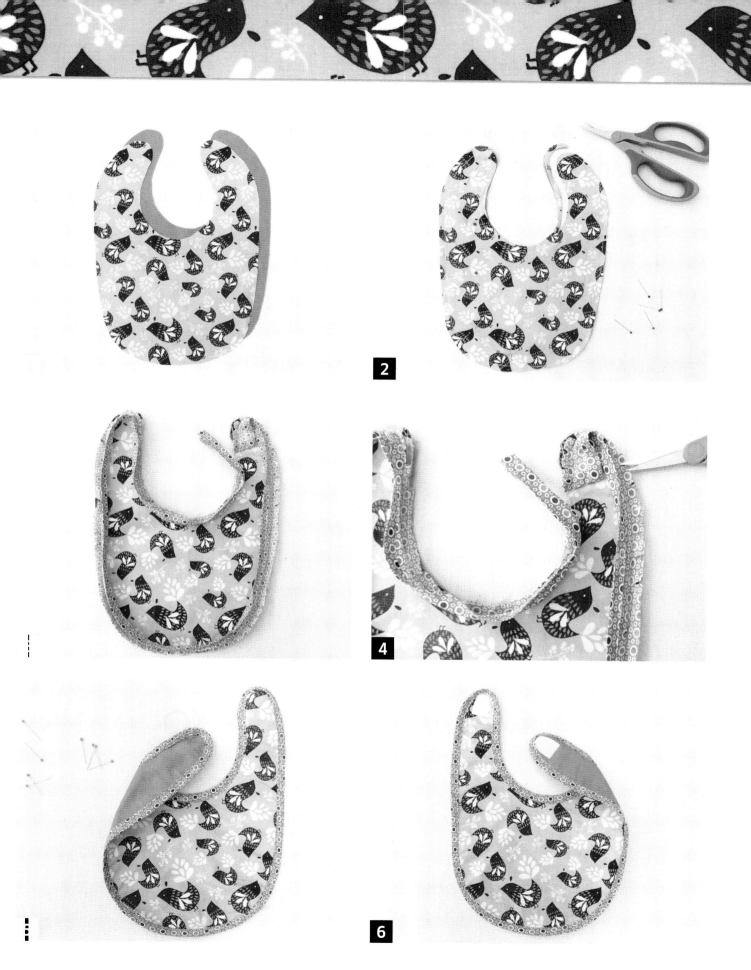

2

4

6

PILLOWCASE DRESS

This design of dress is often known as a pillowcase dress because this simple garment was traditionally made from an old pillowcase. The pattern is for a six-month-old baby, but you can adapt it to make the dress for an older child if you have more fabric.

Find the template on page 131

You will need
1 fat quarter of fabric
40in (1m) length of 1in (2.5cm)-wide ribbon
Pencil
Tracing paper or baking parchment
Pins
Tape measure or ruler
Scissors
Dress-making scissors
Sewing machine
Thread to match fabric
Iron and ironing board
Sewing needle
Safety pin

1 Photocopy the template on page 131 and trace over it onto tracing paper or baking parchment. Cut out with paper-cutting scissors to make a pattern. Fold the fabric in half, pin the pattern to the fabric and cut out.

2 With right sides facing, pin and machine sew the side seams with a straight stitch (see page 14), using a ⅜in (1cm) seam allowance. Press the seams open.

3 Pin one side of the bias binding to the wrong side of one armhole and machine sew in place. Trim and cut notches in the seam (see page 15). Fold the bias binding over to cover the edge of the armhole, press then use a needle and thread to sew down. Repeat for the other armhole. See also Bias Binding technique, page 16.

4 To make the casing for the ribbon, fold over the top edge of the dress by ⅜in (1cm), press, then fold down by a further 1in (2.5cm). Using a straight stitch, machine sew down close to the edge, then repeat on the other side.

5 Turn right side out. Pin the hem to the length you want then machine sew around the hem close to the edge.

6 Using the safety pin, thread the ribbon through the casing, and tie the end in a bow on one shoulder. Press the garment to finish.

Tip

To neaten the raw edges on the side seams, use a zigzag stitch before sewing the seams together.

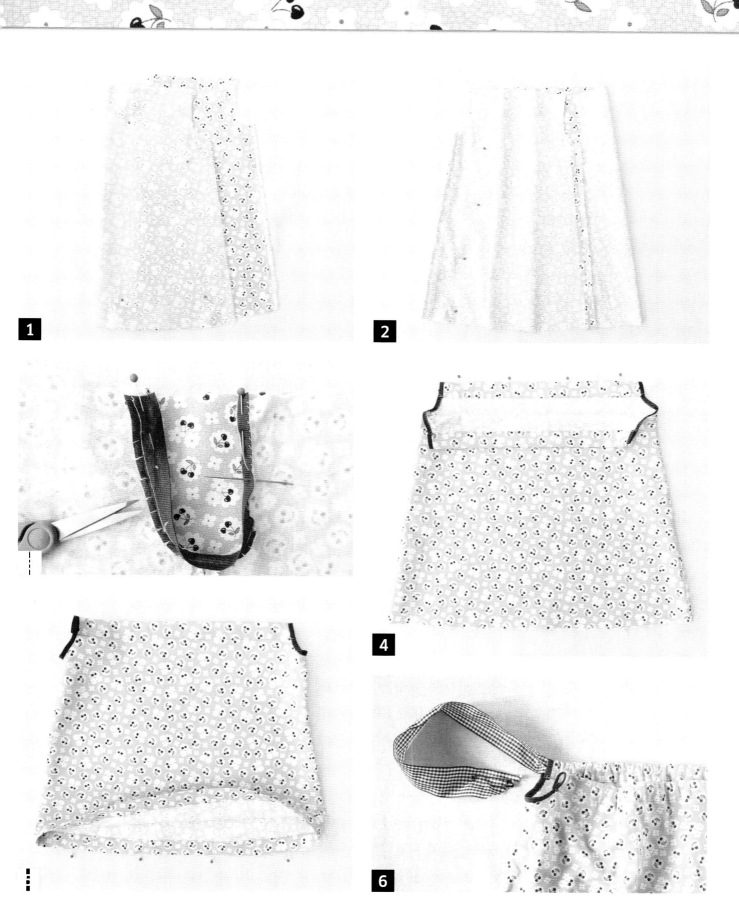

BOOK BAG

Every schoolchild needs a book bag, and a home-made one is less likely to get lost in class. It's best to use a durable fabric, or you could line the bag with calico to make it more substantial. This would also be good to use as a gym bag.

You will need
2 fat quarters of main fabric
6 x 2in (15 x 4cm) of contrast fabric
120in (3m) length of cord
Tape measure or ruler
Dress-making scissors
Iron and ironing board
Pins
Large safety pin
Sewing machine
Thread to match fabric
Sewing needle (optional)

Tip
You could sew this fairly quickly by hand using a running stitch, if you don't have a sewing machine.

1 Cut two rectangles measuring 15 x 10in (38 x 25cm) from the main fabric.

2 To make the loops, fold the strip of contrast fabric in half lengthways. Press flat. Open up and fold each raw edge to the line just made with the iron. Fold in half again so all the raw edges are hidden. Pin and machine sew with a straight stitch (see page 14) close to the edge. Fold the strip in half widthways and cut in half to make two pieces 3in (7.5cm) long for the loops.

3 Measure ¾in (2cm) from the right side of the bottom of the bag front. Pin the loops on each side so they face inwards. With right sides facing, pin the bag front on top of the bag back, sandwiching the loops in between. See also Hanging Loop, page 17.

4 Start machine sewing the front of the bag to the back, starting 2½in (6.5cm) from the top of one side, stitching along the bottom edge and finishing 2½in (6.5cm) from the top of the other side. Use a ⅜in (1cm) seam allowance. Clip a notch up to the seam where the stitching ends on both sides.

5 To neaten, fold, press and then sew along the unsewn side seams, top front and back edges.

6 Turn the top edges under by 1⅜in (3.5cm), pin and press flat. This will be the casing for the drawstring cords. Machine sew with a straight stitch or hand sew with a running stitch (see page 15).

7 Using the safety pin, thread one of the cords through the front and back casing. Thread the second cord through the front and back casing, starting from the opposite side to the first cord. Pass the cords through the loops and knot the ends.

2

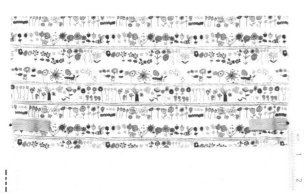

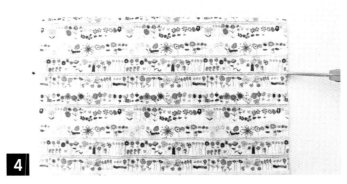

4

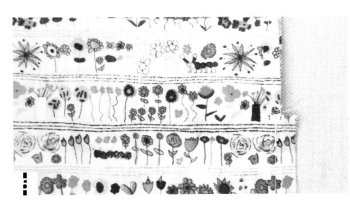

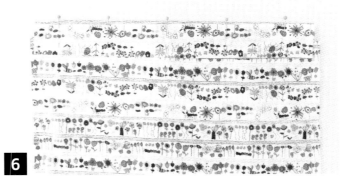

6

Tip

If you're patching pieces of fabric together, add extra material for the seam allowances – at least ³⁄₈in (1cm) all round for each piece used in the patching process.

BABY BLOOMERS

These beautiful bloomers are a great way to cover up unsightly nappies, and are suitable for both boys and girls. The elasticated waist makes them comfortable for the baby to wear and you will find them easy to get on and off when it's time to change the nappy.

Find the templates on pages 132–133

You will need
2 fat quarters of fabric
36in (91cm) length of elastic
Pencil
Tracing paper or baking parchment
Tape measure or ruler
Scissors
Pins
Iron and ironing board
Sewing machine
Thread to match fabric
Sewing needle
Dress-making scissors
Large safety pin

1 Photocopy the templates on pages 132–133 and trace over them onto tracing paper or baking parchment. Cut out with paper-cutting scissors to make the patterns. Pin the patterns onto the fabric and cut out two of each.

2 With right sides facing, pin the bloomer fronts together and machine sew down the centre seam with a straight stitch (see page 14). Repeat with the centre back pieces. Press the pieces flat.

3 With right sides together, pin the front of the bloomers to the back and machine sew down the inside and outside leg seams, using a ⅜in (1cm) seam allowance throughout.

4 To make the elastic casing for the waist, turn down the top edge by ⅜in (1cm), press, then turn down by a further 1in (2.5cm). Press, pin and machine sew. Repeat at the bottom of the bloomer legs.

5 For the waistband elastic, measure the baby's waist and add 1in (2.5cm) for joining the ends. Unpick a few stitches on the inside of the waistband seam. Using the safety pin, thread the elastic into the casing.

6 Hand sew the ends of the elastic together, then slip stitch the seam opening closed (see page 15). Repeat for the elastic in the legs.

Tip

To neaten the edges, use zigzag stitch down the centre, inside and outside leg seams.

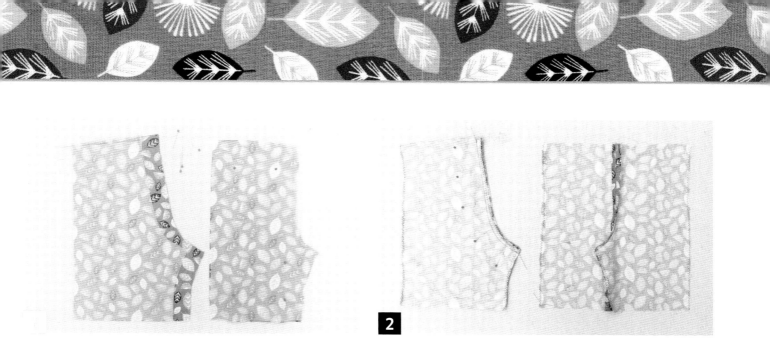

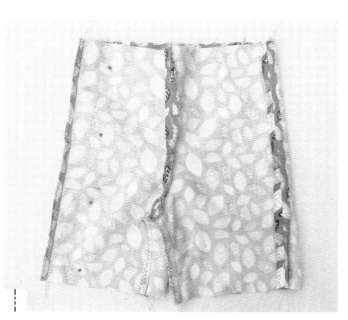

2

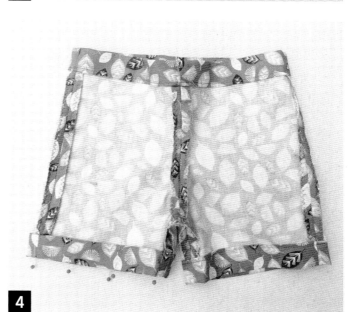

4

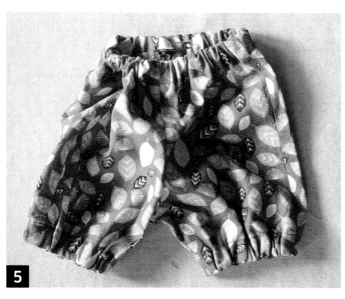

5

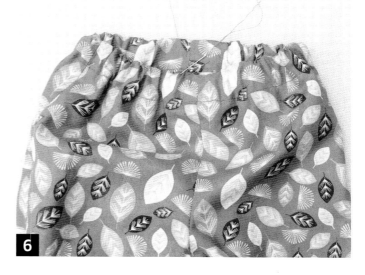

6

CAT CUSHION

Who can resist a cute feline cushion like this? The unusual shape and striking features transform this project from an ordinary cushion into something special for an older child's room. You can use a less expensive plain fabric or calico for the back.

Find the templates on pages 134–135

You will need
2 fat quarters of fabric
5 x 5in (13 x 13cm) of felt
5 x 5in (13 x 13cm) of double-sided fusible webbing
8oz (225g) polyester wadding
2 small white beads for pupils (optional)
Tracing paper or baking parchment
Pencil
Scissors
Tape measure or ruler
Pins
Dress-making scissors
Sewing machine
Thread to match fabric
Sewing needle
Iron and ironing board

Note: This cushion is decorative and must not be given to babies or young children.

1 Photocopy the templates on pages 134–135 and trace over onto tracing paper or baking parchment. Cut out with paper-cutting scissors to make the patterns. Fold the main fabric in half. Pin the paper pattern for the cat's face onto the fabric and cut out two cat faces.

2 Draw the face details onto the paper side of the double-sided fusible webbing then press to fuse them onto the felt. Cut around the edge of the facial features.

3 Peel the backing paper off the facial features and arrange them on the right side of the fabric. Press to fuse onto the fabric. Add a line of machine stitching using straight stitch (see page 14) to secure the features firmly to the cushion.

4 With right sides together, pin and machine sew around the edge of the cushion using a ⅜in (1cm) seam allowance and a straight stitch. Leave an opening of 2¾in (7cm) in the seam between the ears for turning. Trim the seam and cut notches in the curved edges (see page 15).

5 Turn right sides out through the opening in the seam. Fold in the edges of the opening and press the seams flat. Fill the cushion with toy stuffing or wadding.

6 Slip stitch (see page 15) the opening closed with a needle and thread. Sew on two white beads to make pupils for the eyes if you wish.

Tip

Sometimes to make a pattern fit on a scrap of fabric you will have to cut on the cross. To stabilize and reduce stretch, press fusible webbing onto the reverse side of the outer fabric.

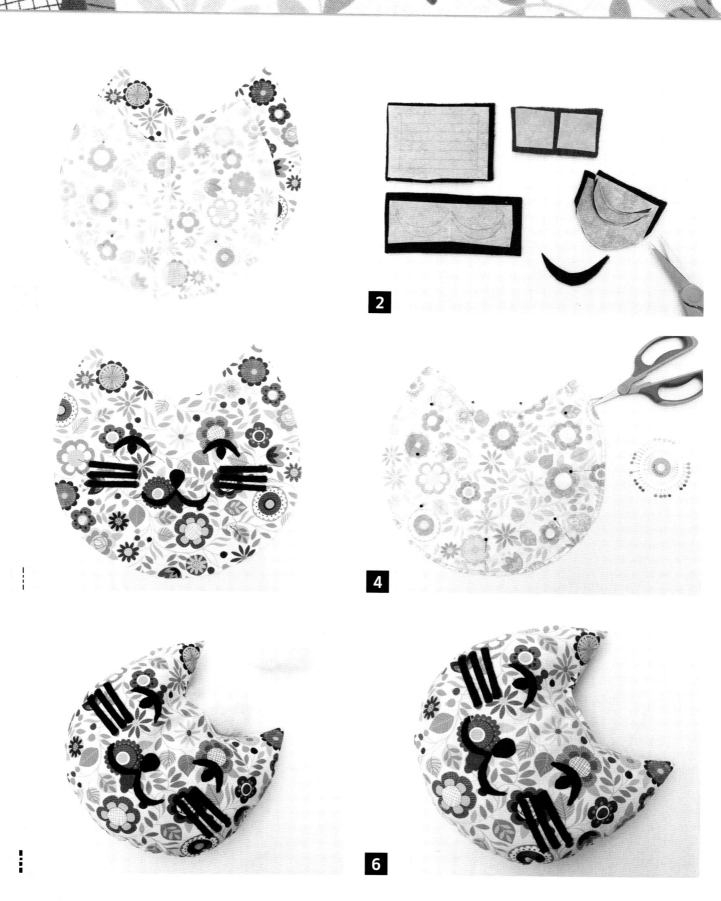

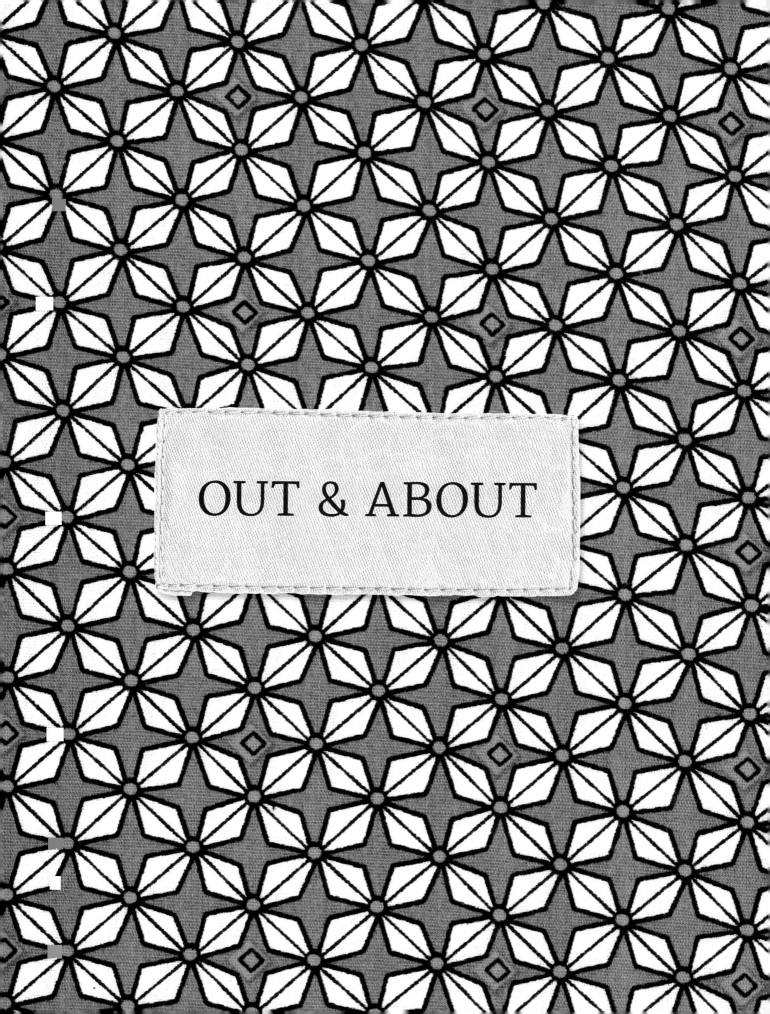

OUT & ABOUT

TENT TIDY

There are never enough pockets in a tent. Keep the essentials of camping life such as your book, glasses, torch and insect repellent close to hand in this neat tent tidy. It has several useful pockets and you can hang it up in the tent to keep it within easy reach.

You will need
2 fat quarters of main fabric for the backing and lining
2 fat quarters of contrast fabric for the pockets and hanging loop
9 x 18in (23 x 46cm) of fusible interfacing
Tape measure or ruler
Sewing machine
Thread to match fabric
Sewing needle
Iron and ironing board
Pins
Dress-making scissors
Water-erasable pen

1 From the main fabric, cut two rectangles 9 x 18in (23 x 46cm). From the contrast fabric, cut three rectangles: 9 x 11in (23 x 28cm), 9 x 7in (23 x 18cm) and 9 x 6in (23 x 15cm), and a strip measuring 8 x 3in (20 x 7.5cm) for the hanging loop. Iron the fusible interfacing onto the reverse of one of the pieces of main fabric.

2 To make the pockets, fold each piece of fabric in half lengthways, with reverse sides facing, and press. Pin the largest pocket in place at the lower edge of the backing fabric. Machine sew the pocket around three sides with a ¼in (6mm) seam allowance using straight stitch (see page 14), leaving the top long edge open.

3 To position the middle pocket, measure 8in (20cm) up from the base, and place the long folded edge of the middle pocket so that it is pointing downwards. Pin and machine sew along the other long edge using a ⅜in (1cm) seam allowance. Repeat with the smallest pocket 13in (33cm) from the base.

4 Press both pockets upwards so the long folded edge points towards the top of the tent tidy. Pin and sew down the two short sides with a ¼in (6mm) seam. To divide the central pocket into two, sew a line in the middle through the pocket and backing. Use a water-erasable pen to mark the smallest pocket into three, and stitch along both lines.

5 To make the hanging loop, with right sides out, fold the strip of loop fabric in half lengthways. Press the fold to crease. Open out the fabric and fold in the outside edges to meet on the crease. Press to crease. Fold the strip in half again so all the raw edges are hidden. Pin and sew along the turned edge to close. See also Hanging Loop, page 17.

6 Fold the loop in half. Pin it at the top of the backing fabric in the middle, facing inwards.

7 With right sides together, pin the other piece of main fabric to the pocket backing fabric. Sew along all the sides with a ⅜in (1cm) seam allowance, leaving an opening of 3in (7.5cm) along the bottom edge for turning through. Clip the corners and seams.

8 Turn through the seam opening. Press the seams and slip stitch (see page 15) the opening closed using a needle and thread.

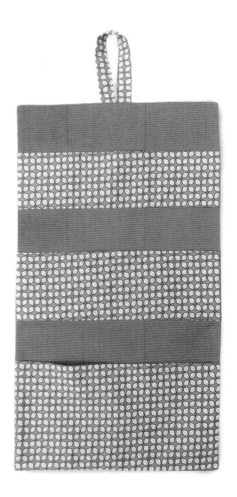

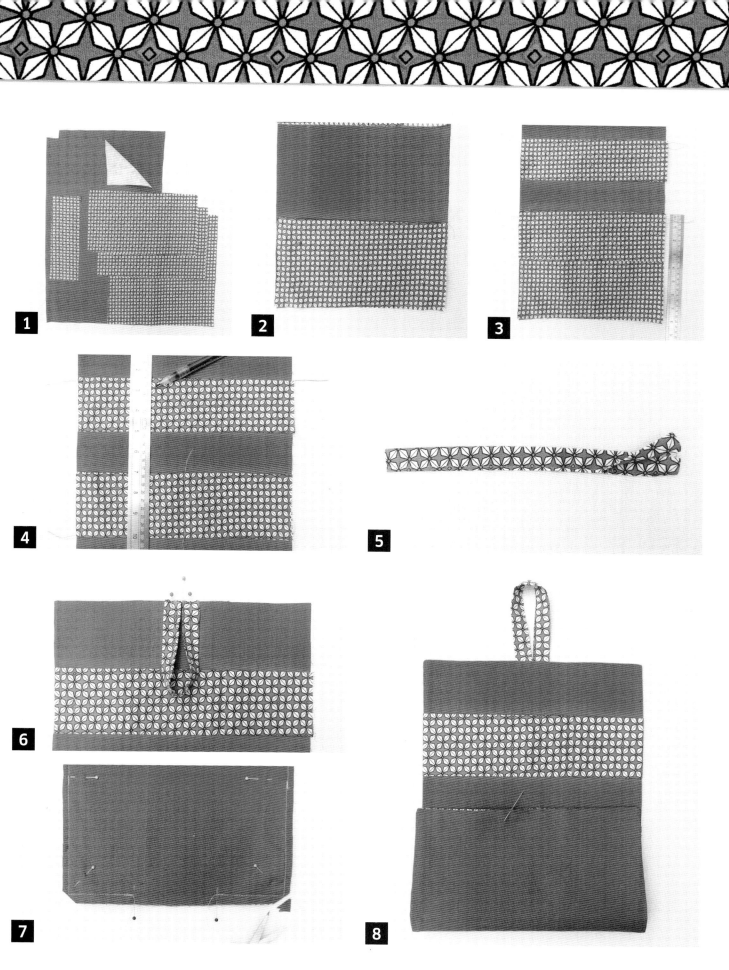

BUNTING

Even little scraps of fabric can be made into something special. The bobble fringe and rectangular shape make this brightly coloured bunting stand out from the crowd. Wherever you hang it, indoors or out, it's sure to bring festival magic to any occasion.

You will need
A variety of small pieces of fabric,
     at least 4½ x 2¾in (12 x 7cm) each
Bias binding, 3½in (9cm) length per piece of bunting
Bobble fringe, 3in (7.5cm) length per piece of bunting
Thin card
Tape measure or ruler
Pencil
Water-erasable pen
Pins
Scissors
Dress-making scissors
Iron and ironing board
Sewing machine
Thread to match fabric

NOTE: One fat quarter will make at least fifteen flags, but there's no need to use the same fabric on both sides.

1 For the flag shape, cut out a template from thin card measuring 4½ x 2¾in (12 x 7cm), using paper-cutting scissors. Draw around the edge onto your fabric scraps, using the water-erasable pen, then cut out the fabric using dress-making scissors.

2 With right sides facing, pin together two rectangles of fabric in different designs. Machine sew around the two long sides and one short side using a ⅜in (1cm) seam allowance and a straight stitch (see page 14). Leave one short side open.

3 Clip the corners (see page 15), then turn the flag right sides out and press.

4 Measure the bottom edge of the flag and cut a length of bobble fringe to fit. Pin then machine sew it in place.

5 Insert the flag between the open sides of the bias binding and pin the bias binding closed, sandwiching the flag. Repeat steps 2–5 to make more flags. Pin the remaining flags in place, 1¼in (3cm) apart.

6 Machine sew along the edge of the bias binding to close and anchor the flags.

Tip

If you are short of time, you could cut out the flags with pinking shears and make them from a single thickness of fabric.

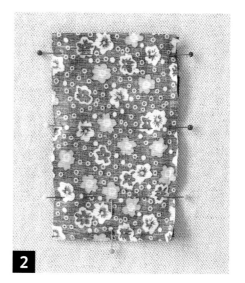

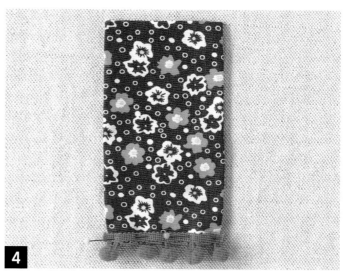

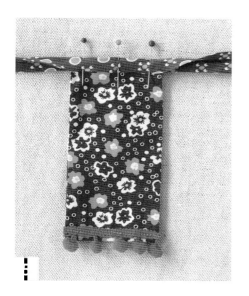

TRAVEL SEWING KIT

It's always useful to have a small sewing kit with a needle and thread for those emergency repairs when you're away from home. You could make a couple of these handy little kits and keep them in your luggage at all times.

You will need
1 fat quarter of main fabric
1 fat quarter of lining fabric
12 x 9in (30 x 23cm) of fusible interfacing
2½in (6.5cm) piece of elastic in a contrast colour to main fabric
¾in (2cm) button
Tape measure or ruler
Pencil, tracing paper or baking parchment
Scissors
Dress-making scissors
Pins
Iron and ironing board
Sewing machine
Thread to match fabric
Sewing needle
Water-erasable pen

NOTE: You can make the whole project from one fat quarter if you use the same material for the lining.

1 Draw two rectangles measuring 7 x 5in (18 x 12.5cm) and 5 x 4in (12.5 x 10cm) onto tracing paper or baking parchment and cut out with paper-cutting scissors to make the patterns. Pin to the main fabric, lining fabric and fusible interfacing, and cut out. Iron the interfacing onto the reverse of the main fabric (the smaller rectangle will form the pocket).

2 Make the pocket. With right sides facing, machine sew the main fabric and lining fabric together along one of the long edges using a ⅜in (1cm) seam allowance and a straight stitch (see page 14). Fold open and press along the seam.

3 With right sides facing, pin the pocket to one of the shorter sides of the main fabric. Stitch along the long edge of the pocket to hold it in place, using a ⅜in (1cm) seam allowance.

4 Make the button loop by folding the piece of elastic in half to form a loop. Pin it to the right side of the main fabric, facing inwards on the side opposite the pocket. See also Elastic Buttonhole, page 16.

5 With right sides facing, pin the lining fabric onto the main fabric and machine sew together using a ⅜in (1cm) seam allowance. Leave a gap of 1¾in (4.5cm) in one of the side seams next to the pocket for turning. Trim the seams and clip the corners (see page 15).

6 Turn right sides out through the seam opening. Fold in the edge of the opening and press. Slip stitch closed (see page 15) with the needle and thread. Fold the holder in two to see where the loop is placed and sew a button so the loop will go over it to close.

Tip

You could use a similar little bag as a credit or travel card holder.

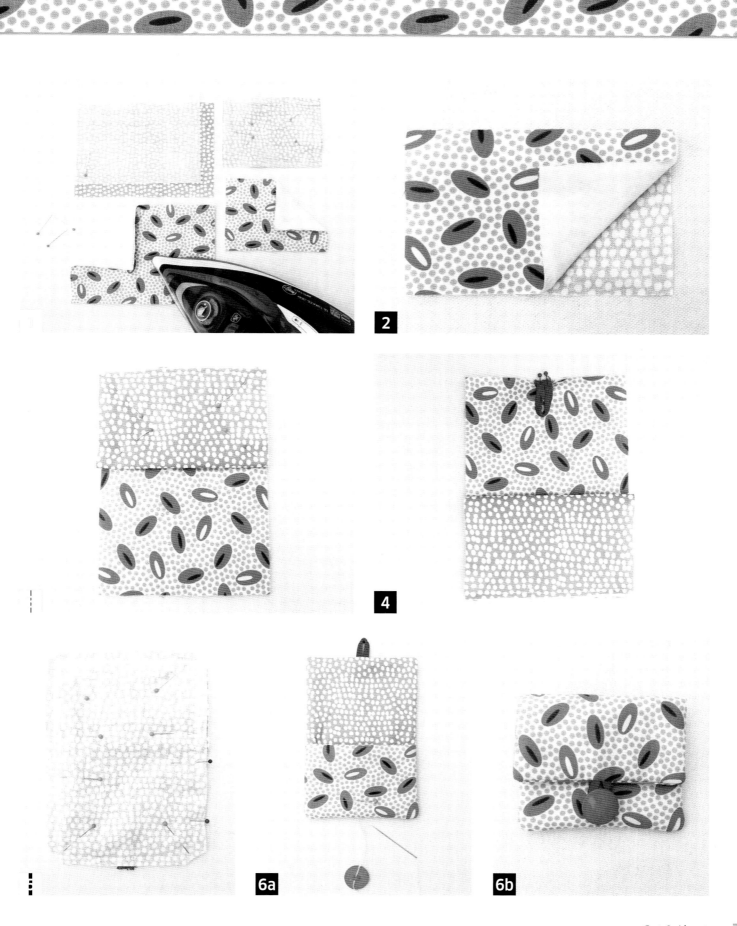

2

4

6a

6b

FESTIVAL FLAG

It's great to have a brightly coloured flag to identify your tent at a festival. Make sure your fabric scraps are machine washable so they will survive the elements, and sew the flag carefully – the back of the flag will be on display as well as the front!

Find the templates on pages 136–137

You will need
1 fat quarter of fabric A
10 x 6in (25 x 15cm) of fabric B
11 x 3½in (28 x 9cm) of fabric C
Tracing paper or baking parchment
Pencil
Scissors
Tape measure or ruler
Pins
Dress-making scissors
Iron and ironing board
Sewing machine
Thread to match fabric
Sewing needle
Bamboo stick

1 Photocopy the templates on pages 136–137 and trace over them onto tracing paper or baking parchment. Cut out with paper-cutting scissors to make patterns. Pin the pattern onto fabric A and cut out one large triangle. Pin the small triangle pattern onto fabric C and cut out. Pin the rectangular pattern for the pole casing onto fabric B and cut out.

2 Fold in the pointed end of the large triangle by ¼in (6mm) and press flat. Fold in the long edges by ¼in (6mm) and then over again by the same amount. Press flat. Machine sew with a zigzag stitch (see page 14) to neaten.

3 Fold in the pointed end of the small triangle by ¼in (6mm) and press flat. Fold in the long edges of this triangle by ¼in (6mm) and press flat.

4 Pin the small triangle on top of the large triangle as marked on the pattern. The folded edges should be on the underside. Machine sew together with a close zigzag stitch along the edges of the two long sides.

5 Add the pole casing as follows. With right sides facing, pin fabric B to the short edge of the flag, starting at point A. Sew to the flag with a straight stitch (see page 14), using a ¼in (6mm) seam allowance. Fold in a ¼in (6mm) hem at the short end of the pole casing nearest to point A. Machine sew with a straight stitch to neaten.

6 Turn in the edges of the remaining long and short side of the pole casing by ¼in (6mm) and press.

7 Fold the casing in half lengthways. Pin and top stitch (see page 17) down along the two long edges and the top short edge, making a tube with a closed top for the pole.

Tip

When sewing the zigzag edges of the triangles, match the top thread to the colour of the fabrics. Match the thread in the bobbin to fabric A so that the back of the flag is neater.

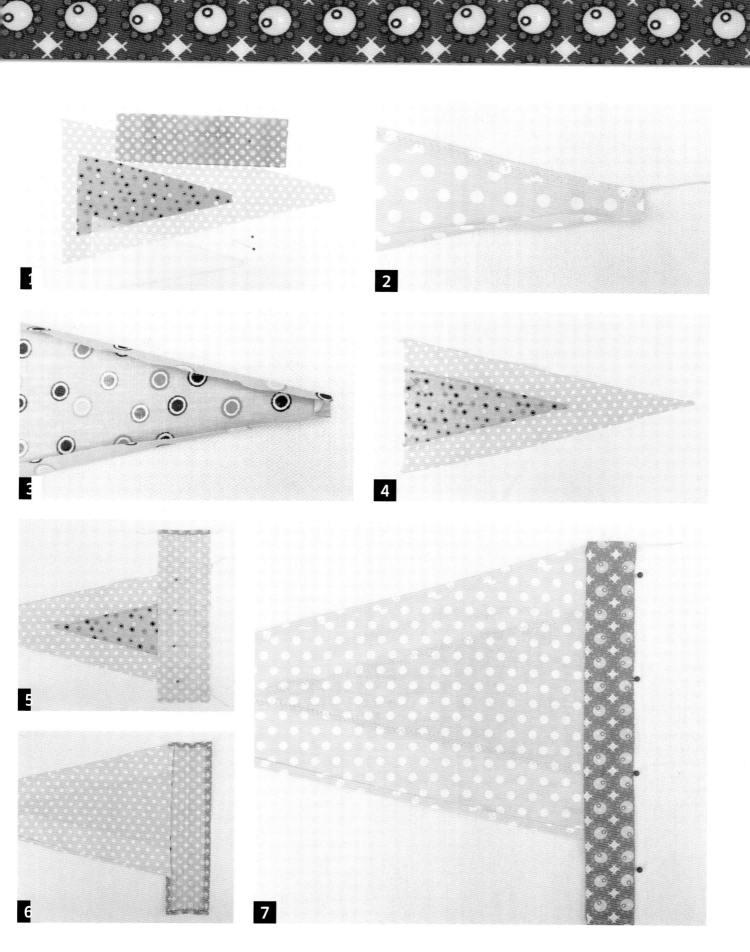

CAMERA-STRAP COVER

Stand out from the crowd with this funky camera-strap cover. Most are wide for carrying over the shoulder and narrow where they join onto the camera. If yours is different, make your own pattern by measuring it and adding a $\frac{3}{8}$in (1cm) seam allowance all round.

Find the template on page 138

You will need

1 fat quarter of main fabric, pieced together to make a strip
  at least 24in (61cm) long and 2½in (6.5cm) wide
1 fat quarter of contrast fabric, pieced together to make a strip
  at least 24in (61cm) long and 2½in (6.5cm) wide
24 x 6in (61 x 15cm) of fusible interfacing
Tape measure or ruler
Tracing paper or baking parchment
Pencil
Scissors
Pins
Dress-making scissors
Sewing machine
Thread to match fabric
Sewing needle
Iron and ironing board

1 Photocopy the template on page 138 and trace over onto tracing paper or baking parchment. Cut out with paper-cutting scissors to make a pattern. Fold the two contrasting fabrics in half and place one on top of the other. Lay the pattern on top, pin together and cut out the two pieces of fabric. Fold the interfacing in half and pin the pattern on top. Cut out two pieces.

2 Press the fusible interfacing to the wrong side of both pieces of fabric.

3 With right sides together, pin then machine sew the front to the back down one long side, between points A on the pattern, using a ⅜in (1cm) seam allowance and a straight stitch (see page 14). Leave a gap of about 3½in (9cm) in the centre (note the marking on the pattern).

4 Machine sew between points B down the other long side using straight stitch. You now have a long, thin tube. Trim the seams.

5 Turn the tube through the opening so that the right side of the fabric faces outwards, then press.

6 Thread the camera strap though the opening. Turn under the open ends of the strap cover and hand sew them onto the original camera strap. Slip stitch (see page 15) the side opening closed with a needle and thread.

Tip

Use a pencil to help turn the fabric the right way in step 5.

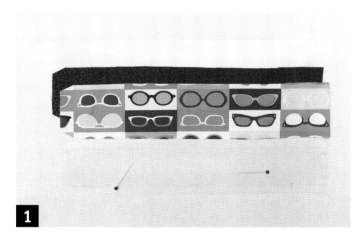

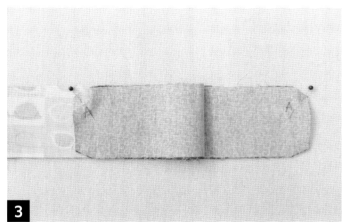

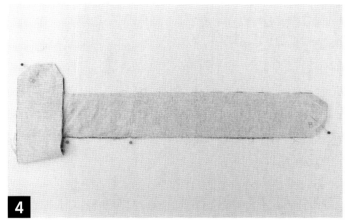

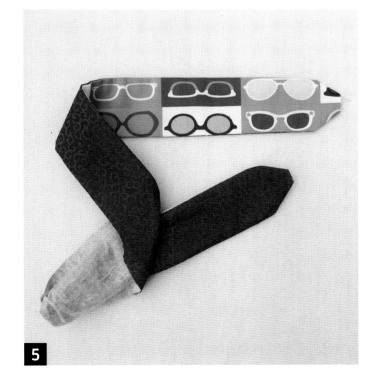

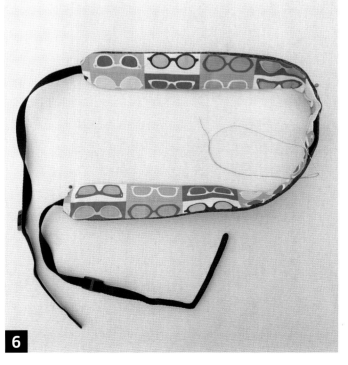

WORKROOM

PIN CUSHION

This bright strawberry makes an excellent pin cushion. It's convenient to use, makes the pins easy to spot and holds them securely. As well as being practical, it's attractive: when you add the pins they look like the seeds of a strawberry!

Find the template on page 139

You will need
1 fat quarter of red fabric
1 fat quarter of green fabric
10 x 10in (25 x 25cm) of fusible webbing
5in (12.5cm) length of ribbon or bias binding for the stalk
A handful of toy filling
Tracing paper or baking parchment (optional)
Pencil (optional)
Tape measure or ruler
Scissors
Pins
Dress-making scissors
Sewing needle
Thread to match fabric
Iron and ironing board
Sewing machine and thread

1 Photocopy or trace over the templates on page 139 onto tracing paper or baking parchment and cut out with paper-cutting scissors to make paper patterns. Fold the red fabric in half, pin on the pattern and cut out two strawberry shapes.

2 Press the green fabric face down onto the fusible webbing. Draw around the leaf pattern twice on the fusible webbing paper and cut out the leaves.

3 Peel off the paper backing. Press a leaf onto each strawberry.

4 Hand sew around the edge of each leaf with a running stitch (see page 14).

5 Fold the ribbon or bias binding in half to form a loop. With the loop facing inwards, position it at the centre of one of the strawberry pieces. See also Hanging Loop, page 17. With right sides facing, pin the other piece of strawberry on top and machine sew round the edge using straight stitch (see page 14) with a 1/4in (6mm) seam allowance. Leave a 2 1/4in (6cm) opening. Trim the seams and clip the curves (see page 15).

6 Turn the strawberry right sides out through the opening and press. Fill with toy filling. Slip stitch (see page 15) the opening closed with a needle and thread.

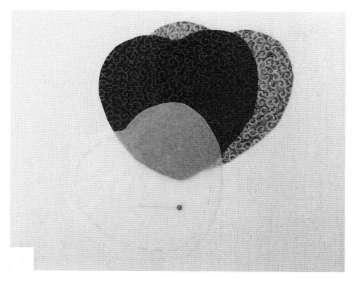

PATTERN WEIGHTS

When you're laying out a sewing pattern on your fabric, pins can warp the pattern and lead to inaccuracies. It's so much more convenient to use pattern weights to hold the pattern in place, and so simple to make your own with fabric scraps.

You will need
8 x 6in (20 x 15cm) of fabric for each pattern weight
Bag of rice
Sewing machine
Thread to match fabric
Dress-making scissors
Pins
Knitting needle
Piece of thin card or small piece of paper
Sewing needle
Tape measure or ruler
Iron and ironing board

NOTE: One fat quarter makes six weights.

1 With right sides together, fold the fabric in half widthways.

2 Pin and machine sew with a straight stitch (see page 14) up the two short sides, using a ¼in (6mm) seam allowance. Leave the top long seam open. Clip the corners (see page 15).

3 Fold out the outer fabric shape to bring the two seams to meet. Press the seams open. Fold in the bottom corners to meet in the centre. Pin and machine sew the top seam, leaving a 2¼in (6cm) opening for turning.

4 Turn the sewing weight right sides out. Prod the corners from the inside with a blunt tool such as a knitting needle and pull at them on the outside with a pin to make them sharp.

5 Make a small funnel by rolling a piece of thin card or paper into a cone. Insert the narrow end of the cone into the opening and fill the weight with rice.

6 Fold under the top edges of the opening and hand sew using slip stitch (see page 15) to close. Repeat steps 1–6 to make as many pattern weights as you wish.

Tip
You could add a fabric loop or piece of ribbon at the top to make it even easier to pick the pattern weight up.

2

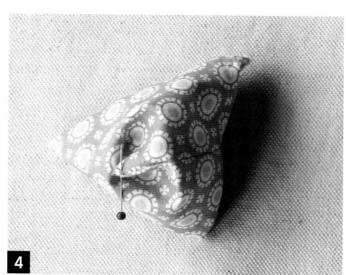

4

5

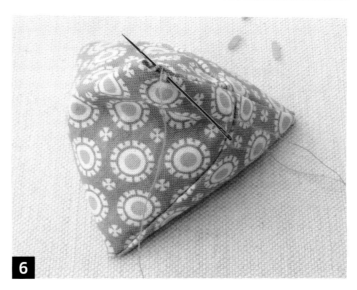

6

PAINTBRUSH ROLL

Protect your brushes and keep them ordered and tidy in this handy artist's paintbrush roll. The neat size and shape makes it perfect for packing up and transporting your kit when you head outdoors for the day to do some landscape painting.

You will need
2 fat quarters of main fabric
1 fat quarter of lining fabric
16 x 13in (40.5 x 33cm) of fusible interfacing
60in (152cm) length of 1in (2.5cm)-wide bias binding
Tape measure or ruler
Tracing paper or baking parchment
Pencil
Scissors
Iron and ironing board
Dress-making scissors
Water-erasable pen
Pins
Sewing machine
Thread to match fabric
Sewing needle

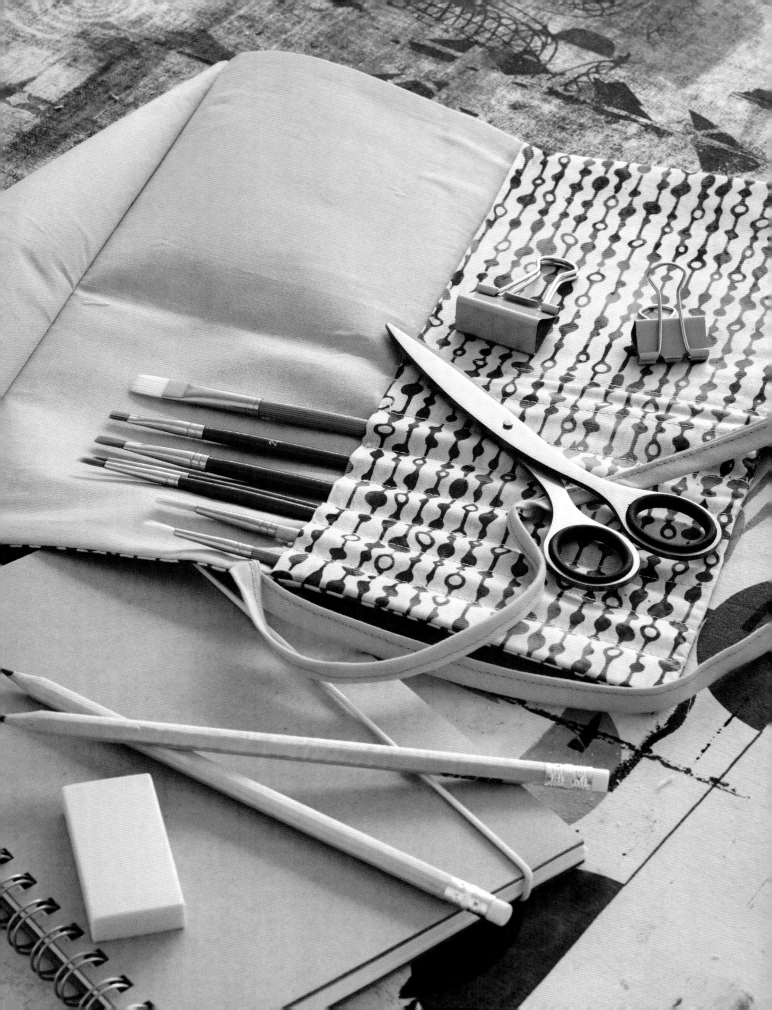

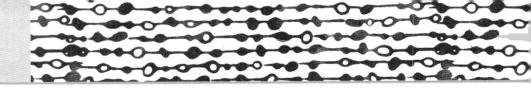
1 Draw two rectangles measuring 16 x 13in (40.5 x 33cm) and 13 x 11 (33 x 28cm) onto tracing paper or baking parchment and cut out with paper-cutting scissors to make the patterns. Pin the larger rectangle to the main fabric, contrast fabric and fusible interfacing, and cut out. Pin the smaller rectangle to the main fabric and cut out for the pocket. Iron the interfacing to the reverse of the lining fabric.

2 With right sides out, bring the two long edges of the pocket together and fold the fabric in half. Press to crease. Starting 1½in (4cm) from the edge, use the water-erasable pen to draw eight channels 1in (2.5cm) apart on the pocket. Leave a large pocket at the end for erasers.

3 Pin and machine sew the pocket along the shorter edge of the lining using straight stitch (see page 14). Sew around three sides with a ¼in (6mm) seam allowance. Machine sew the channels through both fabrics as marked.

4 To make the tie cord, fold the bias binding in half lengthways and machine sew together close to the edge.

5 Fold the stitched bias strip in half and pin the middle of the strip just above the brush pocket on the lining side.

6 With right sides facing, place the main fabric on top of the lining, pin around the edge and machine sew with a ⅜in (1cm) seam allowance. Leave a 3in (7.5cm) opening along the pocket bottom for turning. Clip the corners and trim the seams (see page 15), then turn the project through the opening.

7 Press the seams and slip stitch (see page 15) the opening closed with a needle and thread. Fold down the top edge by 4in (10cm) and add a line of machine stitching ⅛in (3mm) from the fold line to make a flap.

Tip

Trimming a seam allowance reduces bulk and makes the project look more professional. Don't clip up to the seam because there's more chance of the seam coming undone: ⅛–¼in (3–6mm) is about right, depending on the project.

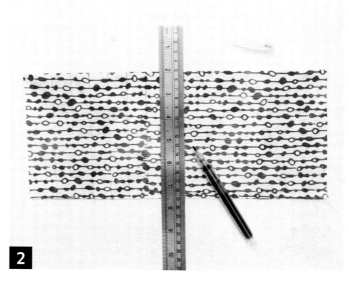

2

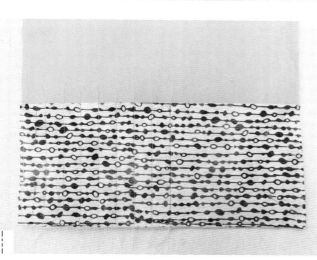

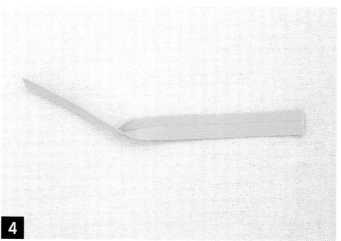

4

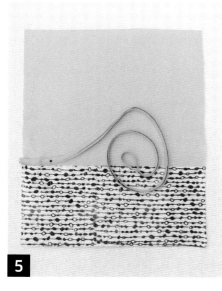

5

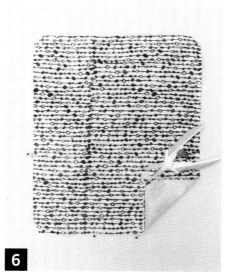

6

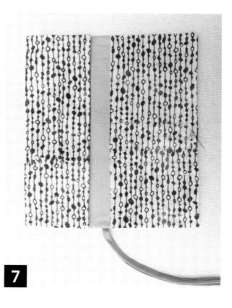

7

KNITTING BAG

All knitters need a dedicated bag for their current project, and this one is a good size.
It's lined to prevent knitting needles poking through and has comfortable handles
so you can take your knitting with you around the house or when on the move.

You will need
2 fat quarters of main fabric
2 fat quarters of lining fabric
2 D handles
Pins
Dress-making scissors
Sewing machine
Thread to match fabric
Sewing needle
Iron and ironing board

NOTE: Use a ⅜in (1cm) seam allowance throughout.

1 Cut two squares measuring 14 x 14in (35.5 x 35.5cm) from the main fabric and lining fabric. With right sides facing, pin the two pieces of main fabric together to make the outer bag. Starting 5in (12.5cm) from the top, machine sew down the side seam using straight stitch (see page 14), then along the bottom and up the other side seam to within 5in (12.5cm) of the top. Trim the bottom corners (see page 15). Repeat with the two pieces of lining fabric to make the inner bag.

2 Turn the outer bag the right way, fold in the open edges of the side seams and press flat. Repeat with the lining fabric but do not turn it the right way round.

3 With wrong sides together, fit the inner bag into the outer one. Turn the open side seams in and press flat.

4 Top stitch (see page 17) both side openings, machine sewing through both the inner and outer bags. Turn down a ⅜in (1cm) hem along each top edge and press.

5 Push the top of the bag through the D handles on both sides, and turn in all the raw edges. Pin in place and hand sew with a slip stitch (see page 15).

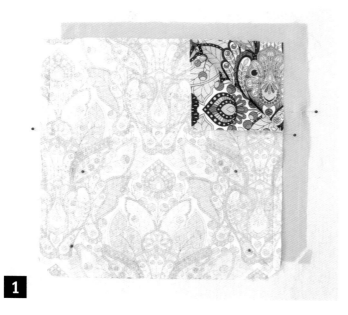

1

2

3

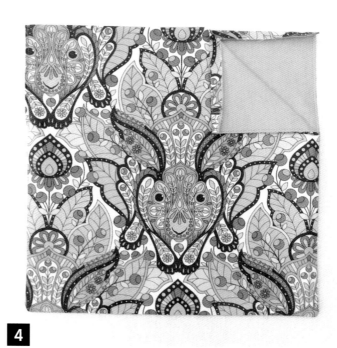

4

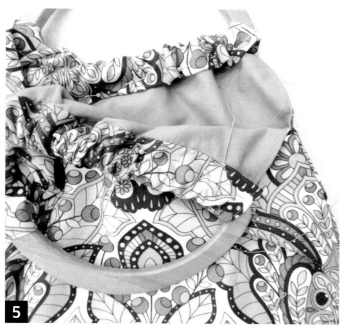

5

Tip

Slide the bulk of the fabric around the handle to make pinning and sewing easier.

PENCIL CASE

This pencil case is lined for durability and fastens securely with a button. You can use the measurements suggested here, or make a larger version to carry around all your stationery essentials, or a slimline version for keeping a few items in your handbag.

You will need
1 fat quarter of main fabric
1 fat quarter of lining fabric
$10\frac{1}{4}$ x 9in (26 x 23cm) of fusible interfacing
2in (5cm) length of elastic
Tape measure or ruler
Iron and ironing board
Dress-making scissors
Sewing machine
Thread to match fabric
Sewing needle
Pins
Button
Water-erasable pen

NOTE: You can make the whole project from one fat quarter if you use the same material for the lining.

1 Cut a piece measuring 10¼ x 9in (26 x 23cm) from the main fabric and the lining fabric. Iron the fusible interfacing onto the reverse of the main fabric.

2 To position the buttonhole elastic, with right side upwards, fold the shorter side of the main fabric in half and mark the centre point on the edge using a water-erasable pen.

3 Fold the elastic in half to make a loop that will fit snugly around your button. Pin and machine stitch it in place with the loop facing inwards using straight stitch (see page 14). See also Elastic Buttonhole, page 16.

4 With the water-erasable pen, mark the reverse of the main fabric on one long side 7½in and 8in (19cm and 20cm) from the bottom edge. Repeat on the opposite side and then on both sides of the lining fabric.

5 To make the pocket, take the main fabric and with right sides together, fold the bottom edge up to the 8in (20cm) mark. Pin and machine sew both side seams with a ⅜in (1cm) seam allowance to the 7½in (19cm) mark. Repeat with the lining fabric, leaving a 2¼in (6cm) opening in one of the side seams for turning.

6 With right sides facing, pin and machine sew together the main fabric and lining of the closing flap and front edge of the pocket. Trim the seams and clip the corners (see page 15).

7 Turn the fabric right sides out through the opening in the side seam. Slip stitch (see page 15) the opening closed with a needle and thread. Tuck the lining inside.

8 Press the seams and sew the button in place on the front of the pocket, ensuring it is in the correct place for the elastic loop.

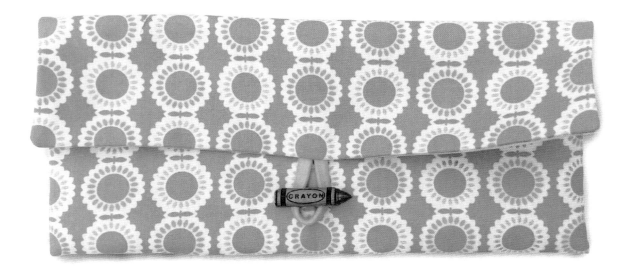

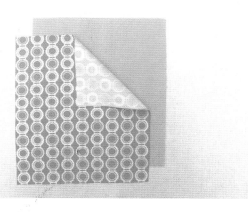

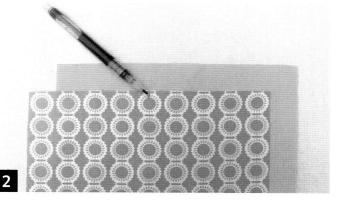

2

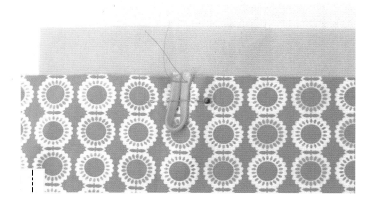

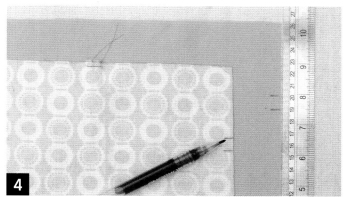

4

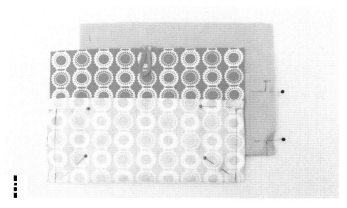

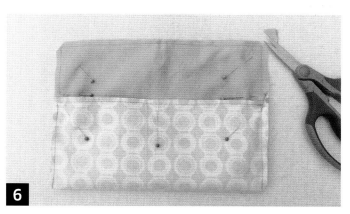

6

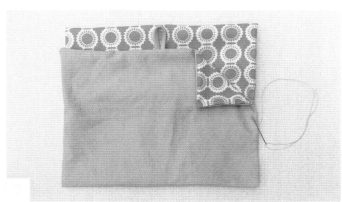

8

PRESENTS

FABRIC FLOWERS

These fun flowers are a very quick and easy way of cheering up a room, especially in the depths of winter. This is a hand-sewn project so you need very little equipment apart from a colourful variety of scraps of fabric.

You will need
2 fat quarters in contrasting fabrics, or 5 x 5in (12.5 x 12.5cm) and
    8¼ x 8¼in (21 x 21cm) scraps for each flower
8 x ⁵⁄₁₆in (20cm x 8mm) green foam ties for the stalks
1 brightly coloured small button per flower
Pencil
Drawing compass or 8¼in (21cm) diameter plate
    and 5¼in (13cm) diameter saucer or similar
Tape measure or ruler
Dress-making scissors
Pins
Sewing needle
Thread to match fabric

NOTE: Two fat quarters will make four flowers.

1 Draw one 5in (13cm) circle on one fabric and one 8¼in (21cm) diameter in a different fabric. Cut out the two circles.

2 Sew a line of tacking (see page 15) ¼in (6mm) from the edge of the larger circle.

3 Draw up the thread to create gathers around the edge of the circle.

4 Pull the thread tight and tie off the ends to create a puff shape.

5 Repeat steps 2 and 3 with the smaller circle.

6 With the flat side of both circles underneath, place the smaller circle on top of the larger one and sew them together in the centre.

7 Sew a button onto the centre of the flower covering up the joins.

8 Sew the stalk onto the back of the flower in the centre.

9 Repeat steps 1 to 8 until you have made a bunch of flowers.

Tip

These versatile flowers can be made into a corsage or attached to a hairband or hairslide.

COVERED BUTTONS

These gorgeous brightly coloured buttons are perfect for jazzing up plain clothes. Make several with the same fabric or go wild and make them all different! A collection of several buttons sewn onto a card would make a lovely gift.

You will need
A variety of small pieces of fabric,
    approximately 2½ x 2½in (6.5 x 6.5cm) each
Small piece of thin card, at least 3 x 3in (7.5 x 7.5cm)
Drawing compass
Tape measure or ruler
Pencil
Scissors
Dress-making scissors
Size 45 (1⅛in/28mm) button-covering kit (see box, overleaf,
    if you don't have one)
Water-erasable pen

NOTE: This is perfect for using up oddments but if you use a fat quarter, you could make more than 50 matching buttons.

1 Make a template for the fabric by drawing a circle of 2¼in (6cm) on the card with the drawing compass.

2 Cut out the card template with the paper-cutting scissors.

3 Draw around the card onto a scrap of fabric with the water-erasable pen, then cut it out.

4 With the right side of the fabric facing down, use the button-making kit and press it into the outer former. Press the domed section of the button onto the fabric.

5 Arrange the pleats of the fabric evenly.

6 Take the button back, and, with the loop for thread uppermost, press it into the domed half of the button.

7 Press the inner former into the back plate to secure the fabric.

COVERING A BUTTON BY HAND

This is how to cover a button if you do not have a kit. Cut out a circle of fabric that is larger than the button. The fabric should be big enough to fold over the back of the button, almost to the middle. Use a needle and thread to sew a loose running stitch (see page 15) round the edge of the fabric circle. Pull the thread to gather, insert the button, then pull the thread tight and secure with a couple of stitches.

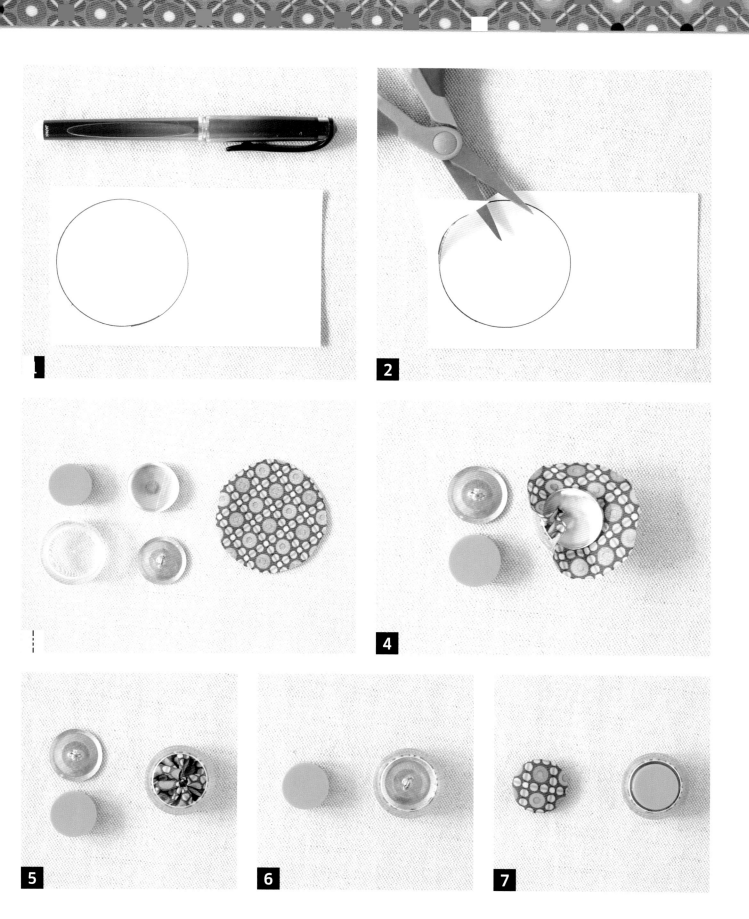

PASSPORT COVER

This cover will protect your passport from getting damaged, as well as making it a less obvious target for pickpockets. It is also a great way to personalize your passport so it doesn't get mixed up with those of your travelling companions.

You will need
1 fat quarter of main fabric
1 fat quarter of lining fabric
21 x 17in (52 x 43cm) of fusible interfacing
Tape measure or ruler
Dress-making scissors
Iron and ironing board
Pins
Sewing machine
Thread to match fabric
Sewing needle

NOTE: You can make the whole project from one fat quarter if you use the same material for the lining.

1 From the main fabric, cut one 8¾ x 6in (22 x 15cm) piece. From the lining fabric and interfacing, cut one 8¾ x 6in (22 x 15cm) and two 6 x 5½in (15 x 14cm) pieces for the pockets. Iron the fusible interfacing onto the reverse of the main fabric and lining pocket pieces.

2 To make the side pockets, fold both pocket pieces in half. With right sides facing, pin the pockets to the shorter sides of the outer fabric, with the folds facing in towards each other, and machine sew in place around three sides, leaving the folded side unsewn. Use a ¼in (6mm) seam allowance and straight stitch (see page 14).

3 With right sides facing, pin the lining fabric onto the main (outer) fabric and machine sew together using a ⅜in (1cm) seam allowance. Leave a gap of 2½in (6.5cm) in the top seam, between the pockets, for turning. Trim the seams and clip off the corners (see page 15).

4 Turn right sides out through the seam opening. Turn the pockets to the lining side, then try the passport for size – it needs to be snug. At this point you can take in the seams if you need to. Press, then fold in the edge of the opening, and slip stitch closed using a needle and thread (see page 15).

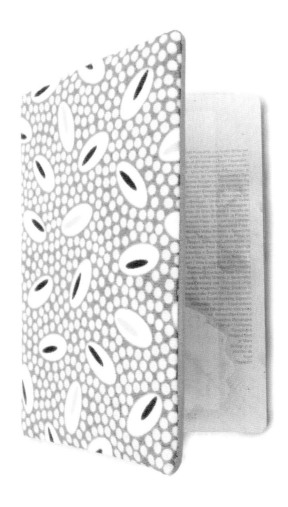

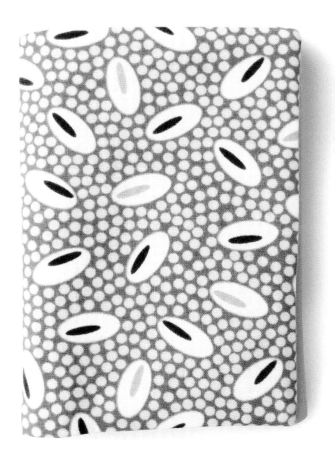

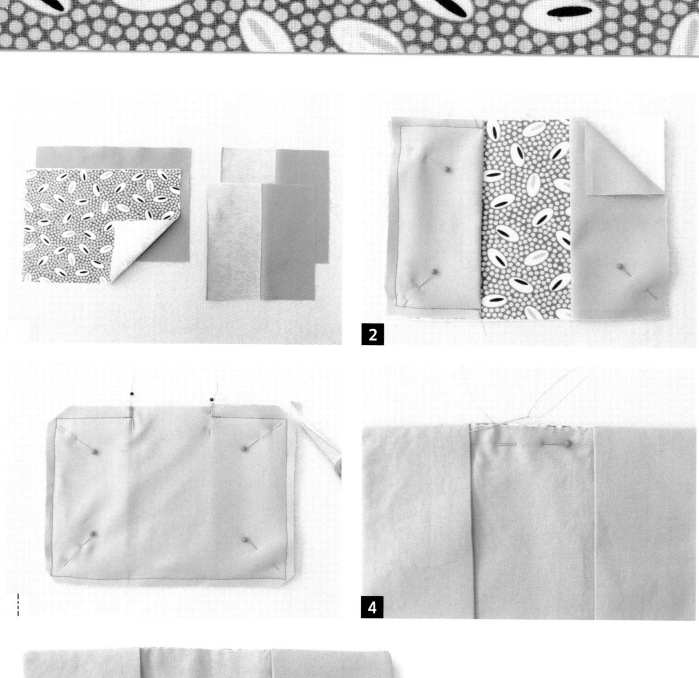

Tip

Use a different fabric to make a passport cover for each member of the family.

GLASSES CASE

There's nothing more annoying than scratching your glasses. Instead, you can slip your glasses or sunnies into a smart little case like this one. This enviable case only takes a scrap of fabric, so spoil yourself and make a matching one to go with every outfit!

You will need
1 fat quarter of main fabric
1 fat quarter of lining fabric
14¼ x 4½in (36 x 12cm) of fusible interfacing
Press stud
Dress-making scissors
Iron and ironing board
Pins
Sewing machine
Thread to match fabric
Sewing needle

NOTE: You can make the whole project from one fat quarter if you use the same material for the lining.

1 Cut a 16 x 4½in (40.5 x 12cm) piece from the main fabric and a 14¼ x 4½in (36 x 12cm) piece from the lining fabric. Iron the fusible interfacing onto the reverse of the lining fabric.

2 Take the main fabric piece and turn in the shorter ends in by ⅜in (1cm). Press to crease, then fold over again by ⅜in (1cm) and press to crease. Unfold the fabric.

3 With right sides facing, fold each strip of fabric in half widthways. Pin and machine sew along the sides with a ⅜in (1cm) seam allowance, using straight stitch (see page 14). Trim the seams and snip off the corners (see page 15).

4 Turn the main (outer) fabric bag right sides out and push the lining inside it.

5 Fold down the top edge of the outer fabric by ⅜in (1cm) along the pressed crease. Then fold again by ⅜in (1cm) on the crease line, covering the top edge of the lining fabric. Pin and hand sew in place using slip stitch (see page 15) and a needle and thread.

6 Using a needle and thread, sew the press stud on the inside of the top edges to fasten.

Tip

If you don't have a press stud, use an elastic loop and button as a fastener.

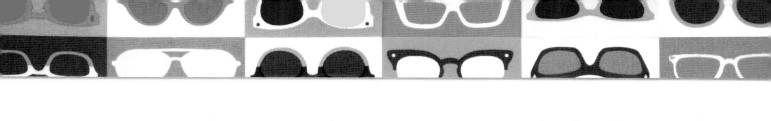

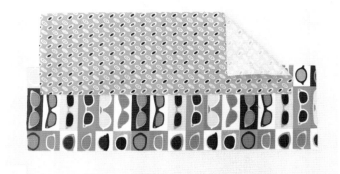

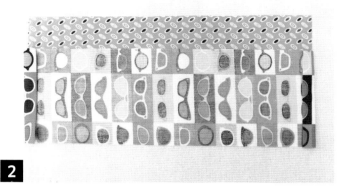
2

4

5

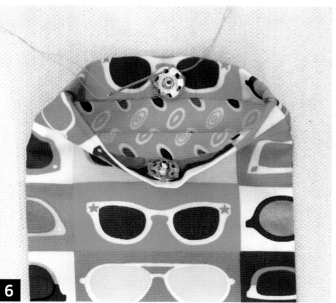
6

MAKE-UP BAG

Here's a nifty bag with handy flexible storage for your make-up, so no more mascara or moisturizer leaking out into your handbag. Simply roll down the top as far as you need to and secure with the ties, to corral all those little items in one place.

You will need
1 fat quarter of main fabric
1 fat quarter of contrast fabric
20 x 17½in (51 x 44cm) of fusible interfacing
Tape measure or ruler
Dress-making scissors
Iron and ironing board
Safety pin
Pins
Sewing machine
Thread to match fabric
Sewing needle

NOTE: In this project the ties were made from another piece of contrast fabric in a slightly different shade of blue, but you can use the same fabric for both the lining and the ties.

1 From the main fabric and fusible interfacing, cut two pieces measuring 10 x 8¾in (25 x 22cm). From the contrast fabric, cut one piece measuring 17½ x 8¾in (44.5 x 22cm) for the lining, and two pieces measuring 1¾ x 21¾in (3 x 55cm) for the ties. Iron the fusible interfacing onto the reverse of the main fabric pieces.

2 To make the ties, fold the long strips of contrast fabric in half and machine sew together with a ⅜in (1cm) seam, using straight stitch (see page 14), to make two tubes of fabric. Use a safety pin to turn the tubes right sides out.

3 Take the two main pieces of fabric, and with right sides facing, pin and machine sew the two long sides together, sandwiching the tie strips in the centre of one of the long seams.

4 Take the lining fabric, and with right sides facing, pin the shorter sides to the shorter sides of the main (outer) fabric. Machine sew the seams using a ⅜in (1cm) seam allowance.

5 Match up the seams, then machine sew the long sides with a ⅜in (1cm) seam allowance, leaving an opening of 2¼in (6cm) on one side of the lining for turning.

6 Trim the seams and cut off the corners (see page 15). Turn right sides out by turning through the side seam opening.

7 Turn in the raw edges of the opening and close with a line of machine stitch. Press the seams.

8 Sew a line of top stitching (see page 17) close to the top edge of the bag.

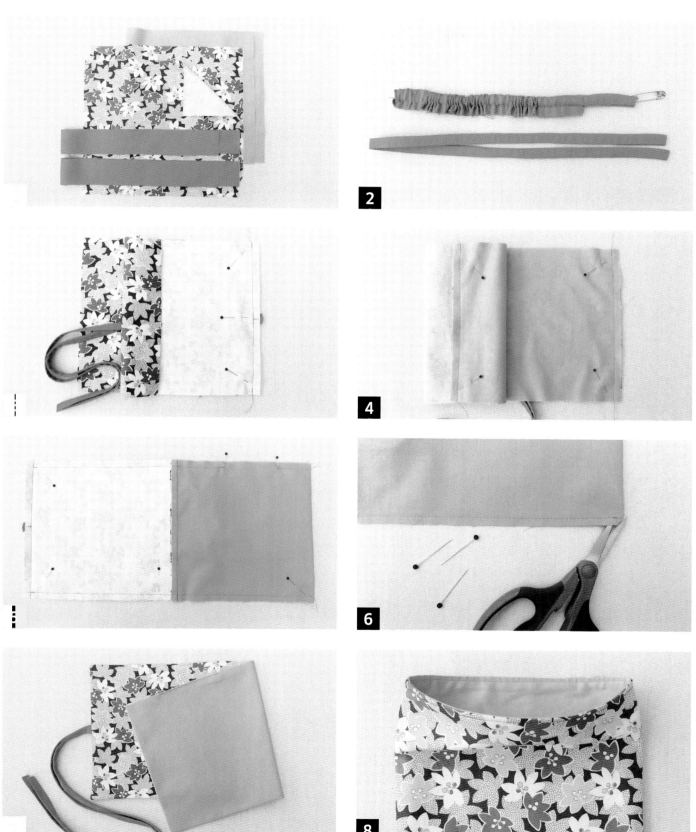

EYE MASK

An eye mask is an essential piece of travel kit for long journeys or camping trips. If you make your own, you can ensure it fits your face perfectly for maximum comfort — and it's quick to make a spare for a travelling companion.

Find the template on page 140

You will need
1 fat quarter of main fabric
1 fat quarter of lining fabric
12 x 5in (30 x 12.5cm) of fusible wadding
22in (56cm) length of elastic
Tape measure or ruler
Tracing paper or baking parchment
Pencil
Scissors
Pins
Sewing machine
Thread to match fabric
Sewing needle
Dress-making scissors
Iron and ironing board

NOTE: You can make the whole project from one fat quarter if you use the same material for the lining.

1 Photocopy the pattern on page 140. Trace over onto tracing paper or baking parchment and cut out with paper-cutting scissors to make a paper pattern.

2 Pin the pattern onto the fusible wadding, main and lining fabric and cut out one of each. Measure the elastic around the back of your head and cut a piece to that dimension plus ¾in (2cm). Iron the fusible wadding onto the back of the main (outer) fabric.

3 Pin the elastic onto the front of the main fabric so the ends point out and sew it into place. (The main part of the elastic is lying against the fabric.)

4 With right sides facing, and the elastic loop in the middle, pin the main fabric to the lining fabric then machine sew with a straight stitch (see page 14), using a ¼in (6mm) seam allowance throughout. Leave a 2¼in (6cm) gap along the top edge for turning. Clip up to the stitching around the curves (see page 15).

5 Turn the mask the right way. Using a needle and thread, slip stitch (see page 15) the opening closed. Press flat, taking care not to iron the elastic because it might melt.

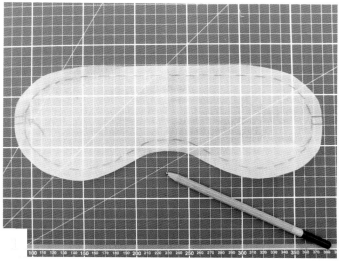

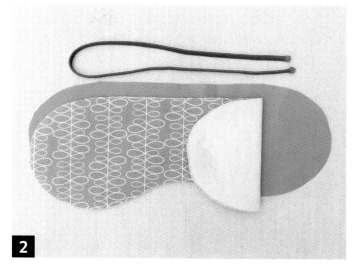

2

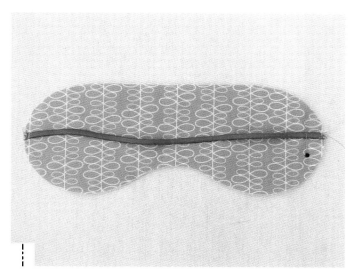

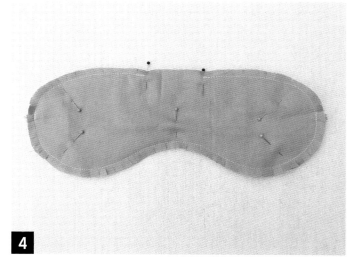

4

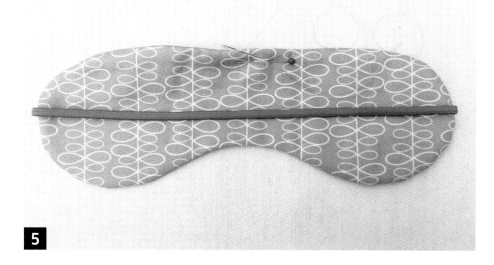

5

Tip

If you can't find nice elastic, buy a long elastic hair tie in a pretty colour and cut it to use instead.

TEMPLATES

Templates that are shown at actual size can be traced and cut out, or photocopied. For templates that have been reduced in size, enlarge them on an A3 photocopier to the percentage stated.

OWL BROOCH
Page 28
Copy at 100%

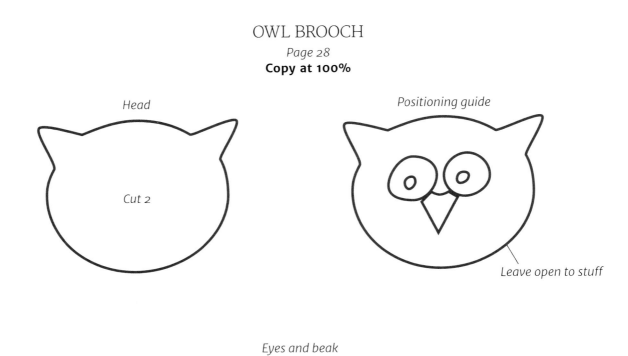

Head

Cut 2

Positioning guide

Leave open to stuff

Eyes and beak

Cut 1

APPLIQUÉ PATCH

Page 32

Copy at 100%

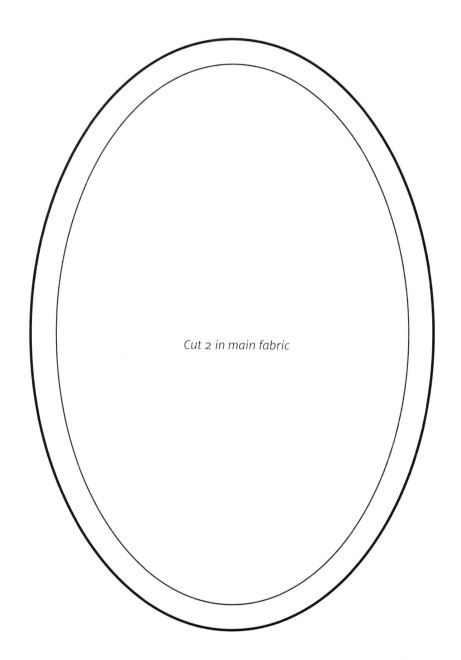

Cut 2 in main fabric

PARTY BIB

Page 38
Copy at 150%

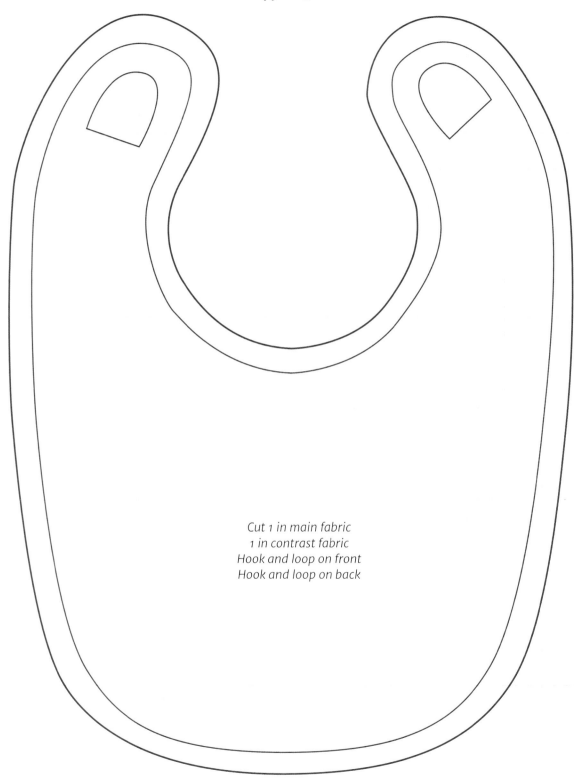

Cut 1 in main fabric
1 in contrast fabric
Hook and loop on front
Hook and loop on back

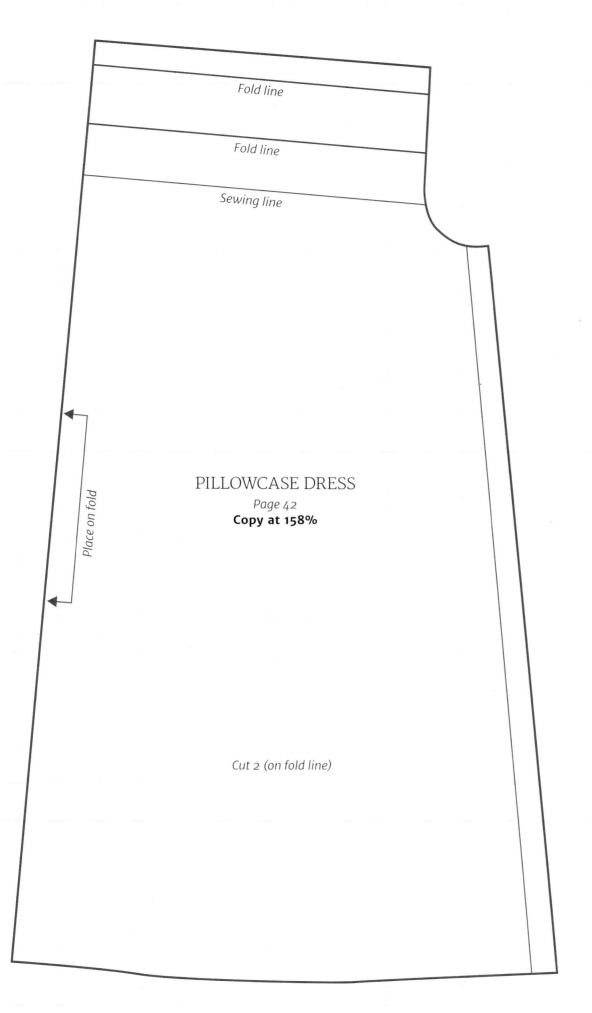

Fold line

Fold line

Sewing line

Place on fold

PILLOWCASE DRESS

Page 42

Copy at 158%

Cut 2 (on fold line)

BABY BLOOMERS

Page 50
Copy at 150%

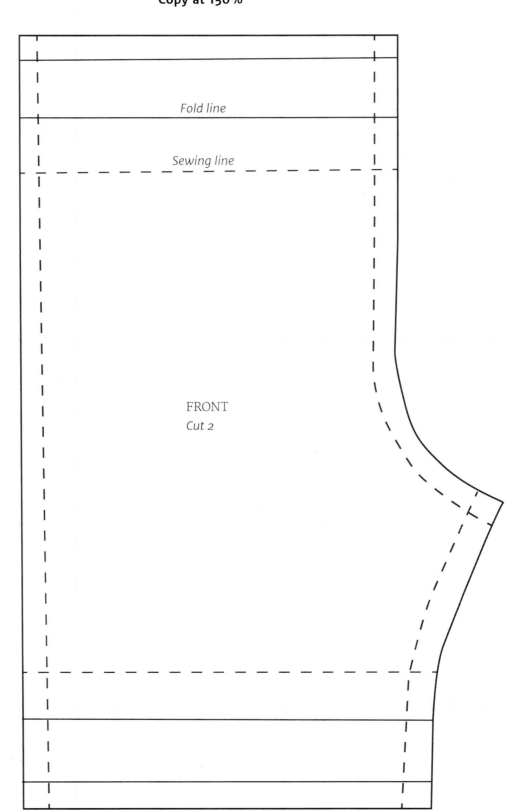

Fold line

Sewing line

FRONT
Cut 2

BABY BLOOMERS

Page 50

Copy at 150%

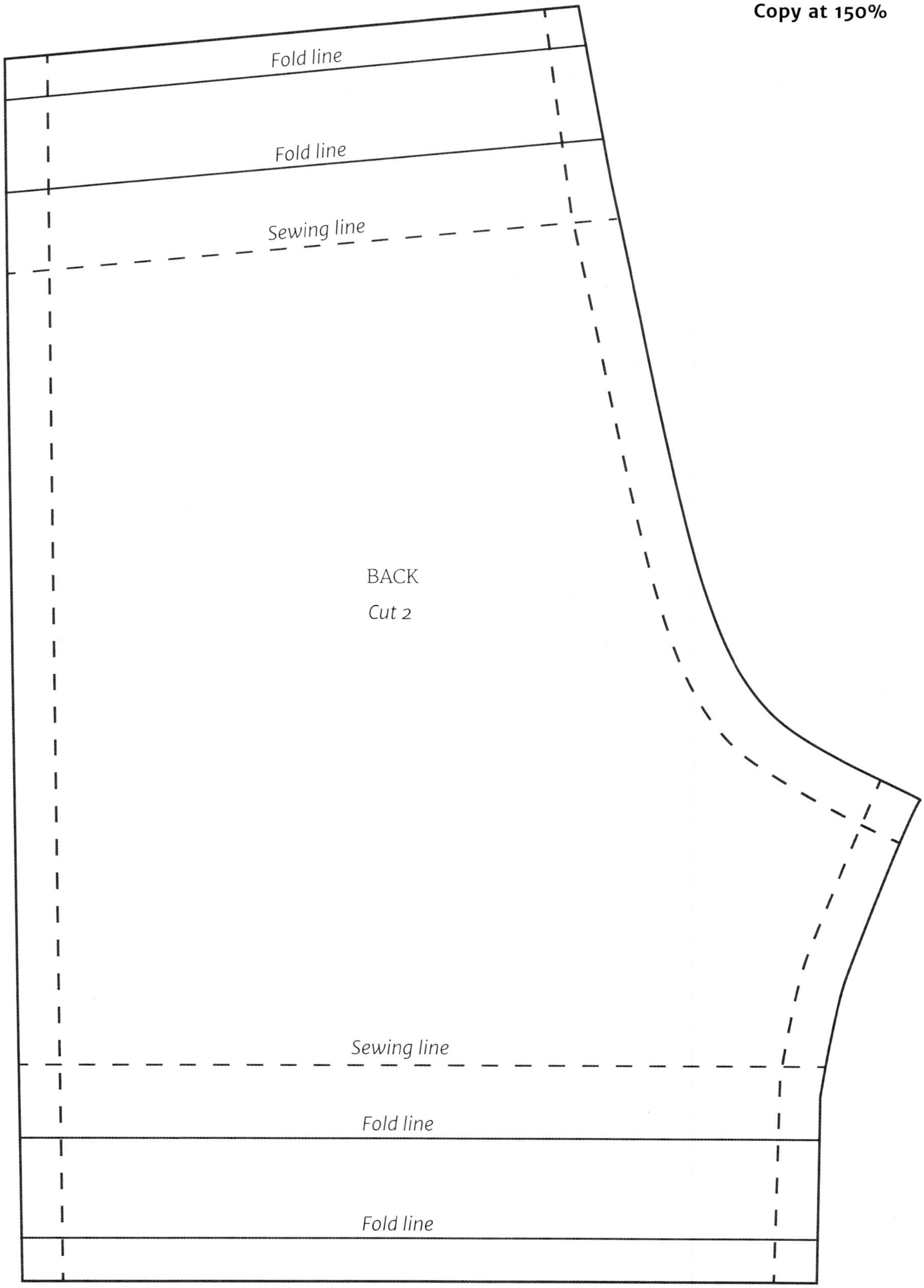
Fold line
Fold line
Sewing line
BACK
Cut 2
Sewing line
Fold line
Fold line

CAT CUSHION

Page 54
Copy at 200%

Cut 2 in main fabric

Sew line

CAT FEATURES

Copy at 100%

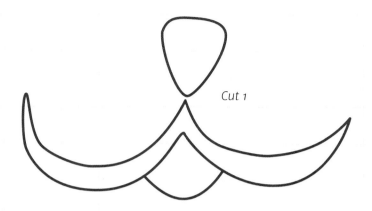

Cut 1

Sew line

Cut 2

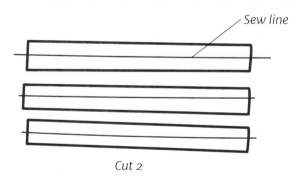

Sew line

Cut 2

FESTIVAL FLAG

Page 72
Copy at 200%

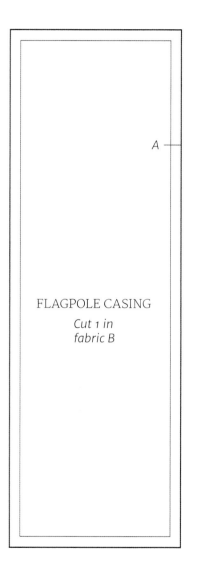

A

FLAGPOLE CASING

*Cut 1 in
fabric B*

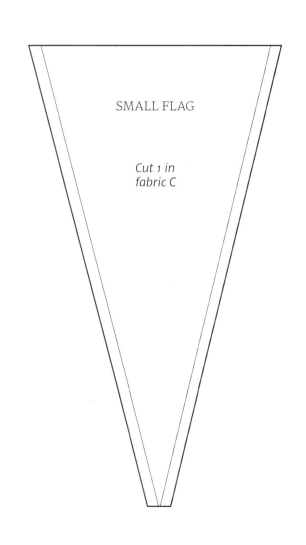

SMALL FLAG

*Cut 1 in
fabric C*

FESTIVAL FLAG

Page 72
Copy at 100%

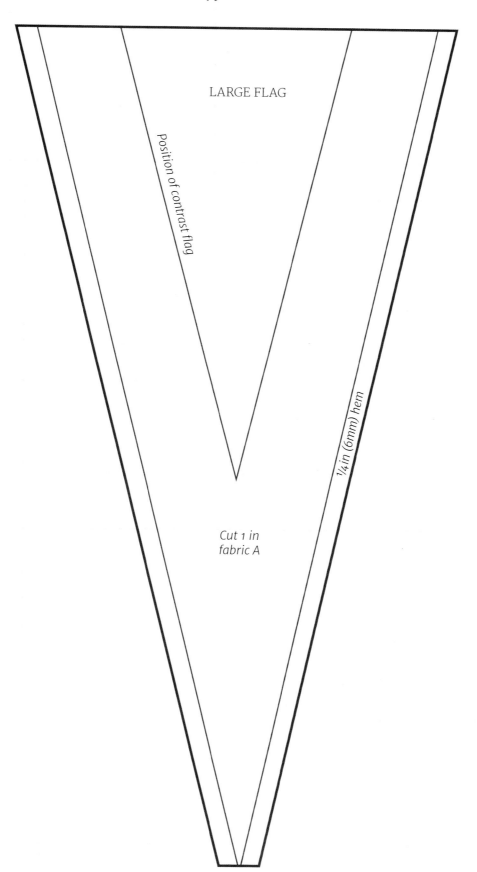

LARGE FLAG

Position of contrast flag

¼in (6mm) hem

*Cut 1 in
fabric A*

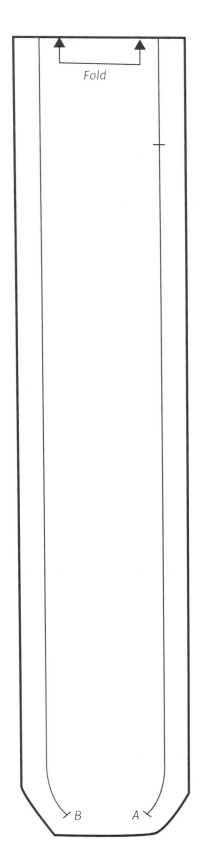

Fold

CAMERA-STRAP COVER
Page 76
Copy at 150%

*Cut 1 in main fabric
1 in contrast fabric
2 in fusible interfacing*

B *A*

PIN CUSHION

Page 82

Copy at 100%

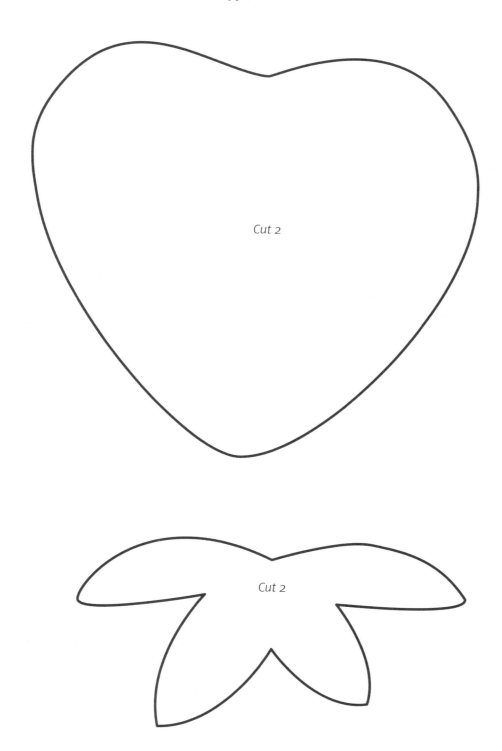

Cut 2

Cut 2

EYE MASK

Page 124
Copy at 150%

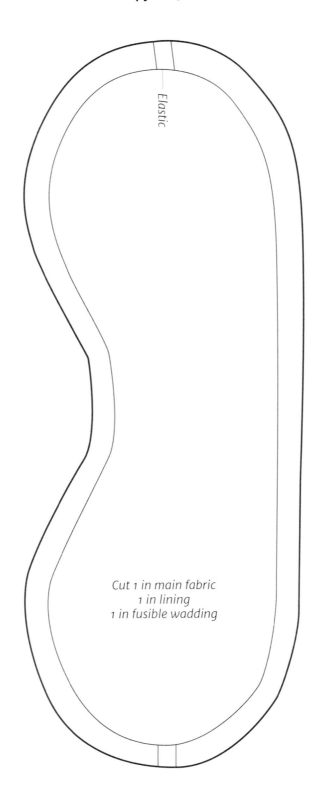

Elastic

Cut 1 in main fabric
1 in lining
1 in fusible wadding

RESOURCES

Scissors
Fiskars
www.fiskars.co.uk

General haberdashery
Korbond
www.korbond.co.uk

Embroidery floss
DMC
www.dmccreative.co.uk

Fusible webbing, fleece,
interfacing
Vlieseline
www.vlieseline.com

Knitting bag handles
Bag Clasps Ltd
www.bag-clasps.co.uk

Sewing machine
Janome
www.janome.co.uk

ACKNOWLEDGEMENTS

We would love to thank everyone who helped us make this book so beautiful, especially our photographer, the inspirational and generous Rowland, who tirelessly made all our shoots memorable and great fun. Also thank you to Gilda, Sara and Jonathan, the publishing team at GMC Publications, who guided and steered us through this project so professionally.

Our special thanks go to our studio team, supportive as ever, the talented Shaz Collier and Antonia Attwood.

Last but not least, thank you to our wonderful, enthusiastic and patient families, who not only put up with our designing and making and creating a mess, but did so with good humour.

INDEX

To order a book, or to request
a catalogue, contact:

GMC Publications Ltd
Castle Place, 166 High Street,
Lewes, East Sussex,
BN7 1XU
United Kingdom
Tel: +44 (0)1273 488005
www.gmcbooks.com